VISIONARIES WITH GUTS

Nancy Matthews

presents

VISIONARIES WITH GUTS

Visionaries Show You Exactly What It Takes, How They Did It and How You Can Too!

Published and distributed by
Visionary Publishing, Inc.
5524 SW 89th Ave
Cooper City, FL 33328
www.VisionaryWithGuts.com
(800) 928-6928

This book is available at quantity discounts for bulk purchases and for branding by businesses and organizations. For further information or to learn more about Visionaries with Guts™, Nancy Matthews and other products and services contact: Nancy@VisionaryWithGuts.com; Web: www.VisionaryWithGuts.com; Telephone: (800) 928-6928

Library of Congress Cataloging-in-Publication Data
Matthews, Nancy
Visionary Publishing, Inc.
Business/Self-Help
ISBN-10: 0615346553
ISBN-13: 978-0-615-34655-7

1 2 3 4 5 6 7 8 9 10

Printed in the United States of America
Edited by: Inspiration Press
Cover Design, Typesetting and Interior Graphic Design by The Third Entity
Cover photo by Megan Matthews
The paper used in this publication meets the minimum requirements of the America National Standard for Information Sciences—Permanence of Paper for Printed Library Materials, ANSIZ39.48-1984.

CONTENTS

Foreword
By John Di Lemme

I am often asked what it takes to step out in faith and take action to live the championship life that you've always dreamed about. Get ready, because you are about to learn exactly how to fulfill your vision through all of the success wisdom right here at your fingertips. I have known Nancy Matthews for many years, and I have personally witnessed her leadership abilities through her speaking, coaching, hosting events and writing this book.

The dictionary defines visionary as someone that sees visions that aren't practicable or realizable. Interestingly, the word guts is defined as: courage and fortitude. Tie those two definitions together and you have Nancy Matthews standing right in front of you. Nancy is someone who believes in you no matter how impossible your dream may seem to others and possesses the courage to empower you to have the guts to go after your dream. Best of all, Nancy practices what she teaches. She didn't hesitate for a second when the divine inspiration hit her to write this book, because she knows that it will change lives.

I know for a fact that this book will be the catalyst that will inspire thousands of people around the world to go after what they really want in life. I encourage you to immerse yourself in the incredible wisdom that lies within the following pages and make the decision to relentlessly pursue your dream.

Preface

Within these pages you will find stories of inspiration, victory, triumph and achievement, shared by a select group of "Visionaries with Guts." Ordinary people, leading extraordinary lives.

This book is offered to spark the flame of the Visionary within you, to add fuel to your fire, so that the special light you were meant to shine will burn brightly and shed light on all the people you are meant to inspire and impact with your unique gifts and talents.

Being a "Visionary with Guts" requires faith, commitment and the willingness to take action. These authors have shared their experiences, their wisdom and their hands-on strategies for creating and living extraordinary lives. This book provides you with the inspiration for creating and supporting the foundation of your extraordinary life and an action plan to ensure your continued success and prosperity as a "Visionary with Guts."

Enjoy the journey, life as a "Visionary with Guts" is a roller coaster ride and the key to happiness is enjoying the ride all the way through; experiencing both the highs and the lows with gratitude, optimism and a passion for living life to the fullest.

Dedication and Acknowledgements

This book is dedicated to my mother, Patricia Carr, who set a clear example of "dancing to the beat of a different drum." As a single mother of four children in the 1960's, she instilled in each of us the values of the importance of family, the pursuit of excellence, self-sufficiency and laughter. Her legacy lives in the spirit of her children who carry the essence of those values.

To my children, Zack and Megan, being your mother is my greatest joy. The highlight of every day is when we're together, sharing love, laughter and our outrageous, silly conversations. Both of you consistently remind me of what's most important. You keep me grounded and humble. To my daughter-in-law, Bethany; it's a blessing to have you in our family. Thank you for sharing your loving heart and gentle spirit. To my grandson, Felix; thank you for providing that perfect ray of sunshine and laughter, sharing the essence of life's simplest pleasures.

To my sisters, Susan and Trish, my best friends, confidants and business partners. I am eternally grateful for your wisdom, perspective and unending belief in me. Your willingness to share this journey, with all its interesting twists and turns is in fact a reflection of the visionary within each of you.

To my brother, Michael, thank you for providing an example of what's possible for all of us. Your accomplishments have served as an inspiration to me.

To my countless friends, mentors and the members of Women's Prosperity Network, thank you. You have each added to this incredible journey and I thank you for your contribution to my life as well as the lives of others. I look forward to continued learning, growing and expansion in the years to come.

To the authors in this book, thank you for stepping up to the plate and contributing to this book and the lives of all who read it. I challenged each of you to participate in this project, with only a two week notice and each of you, being the "Visionary with Guts" I knew you to be, quickly and eagerly responded. You provided exceptional value, and it is my honor to share these pages with you.

To the reader, thank you for having the faith in yourself and this book; to guide and inspire you as you lead an extraordinary life as a "Visionary with Guts."

Introduction

W hat is a "Visionary with Guts?" Where did the phrase come from? What does it mean for you?

Many people have visions, ideas or dreams they think about, few people have the "guts" to take the actions necessary to go for it. Visionaries often take action contrary to popular belief, are the subjects of ridicule and must not only move in a direction against the tide of the masses, they also must overcome their own belief system to step out in faith to fulfill their vision.

My sister, Susan, dubbed me as a "Visionary with Guts" as part of her introduction of me at an event for Women's Prosperity Network. When I first heard her describe me in those terms, I was intrigued and surprised she saw me in that light. I had never really thought of myself in this fashion. I knew my life had been a little different and that I didn't conform to the traditional "play it safe" model. Having a child on my own as a single mother; the purchase of my first dream home which was a foreclosure nightmare (with the roof caved in, moldy wood paneling, flea infested carpeting and 1950's wall paper) saying "Isn't this great?"; starting my own business and then leaving that thriving business to pursue my passion and create Women's Prosperity Network. I've always danced to the beat of a slightly different drummer, I just didn't realize that's what I was doing.

As I reflected on the concept of "Visionary with Guts," I quickly saw that within each of us exists a visionary and that the "guts" comes from having faith, courage and a team of people to support you to bring that inner vision into the light.

So how did I grow from a chubby little girl in Brooklyn with low-self esteem, who was terrified to speak in public to the woman I have become today, confident and excited every time I'm in the front the room? A woman whose greatest joy is to share with others the realization that life is filled with limitless possibilities and that it's our responsibility to share our unique gifts and talents with others. A woman committed to providing value and service to others, setting outrageous goals for herself — and attaining them!

This book outlines the essential ingredients I have found and used to allow me to be a "Visionary with Guts" and offers you the same opportunity. I chose to offer this book as a compilation of many

"Visionaries with Guts," rather than simply coming from my perspective because it is my belief that within each of us there exists a Visionary. A Visionary whose voice matters, whose voice must be shared with others and that each reader will resonate with different teachers, mentors and examples. As you read the chapters you will find bold statements, outrageous ideas and concepts which may be contrary to mainstream thinking. Recognize that each author is in fact a "Visionary with Guts," willing to move forward in the face of fear, ridicule and adversity to share and deliver their vision, truly leading extraordinary lives.

"The only difference between being ordinary and extraordinary is a little bit extra." ~ John Di Lemme

VISIONARIES WITH GUTS

Chapter 1

CREATING THE LIFE OF YOUR DREAMS

"Dreams come true; without that possibility,
nature would not incite us to have them."
~John Updike

Introduction
by Nancy Matthews

Everything begins in thought. When we're children the possibilities are endless, what we want to be when we grow up, where we want to go, what we want to do. For many of us, somewhere along the way we stopped dreaming and became comfortable with what was familiar, secure and reliable. My journey to step out in faith, to walk away from a thriving business and venture into the pursuit of my true purpose and passion, began with a simple thought "You mean I don't have to keep doing this just because I'm good at it? That I have choices and can create a new life path." I then began the process of dreaming again and felt myself come alive. From this place of dreaming and learning to listen to my inner voice and intuition, my life continues to unfold magically!

Give yourself the gift of dreaming again. Dare to step out in faith, ask questions and seek your heart's desire.

Michelle Prince

Michelle Prince is the Best-Selling Author of the book *"Winning in Life Now...How to Break Through to a Happier You!"* She has been endorsed by and worked for some of the most influential, successful motivational teachers and authors in the industry, including Zig Ziglar.

Michelle Prince has embraced personal development, goal-setting and the desire to improve her life since the age of eighteen. Michelle has taken that knowledge to transform not only her own life, but also the lives of millions of people who want to break through to a life of greatness.

Aside from being an author, Michelle is a sought after motivational speaker, one-on-on mentor and radio show host on the "Winning In Life Now Radio Show." She owns her own company, Prince Performance Group as well as her own publishing company, Performance Publishing.

Michelle's style is one who can see your greatness and help you manifest that into action. She will help you to reach higher and go farther with her support and encouragement along the way. Whether you need to be pushed, pulled, inspired, challenged or left alone, Michelle knows just the right steps to help you keep moving toward achieving your goals.

Contact Michelle Prince:
Email: Info@PrincePerformance.com
www.PrincePerformance.com

Believe It to Achieve It
by Michelle Prince

Eighteen months ago, I had a dream. My dream was to become a best-selling author, inspirational speaker and really make a difference in the lives of people all over the world.

The problem was it was just a dream. I had no idea how to make it happen.

In July 2008, a good friend of mine was coming to Dallas to attend a personal development seminar. My friend had created a goals program, which she sold at the seminars. Since my background had always been in sales, and she was a lifelong friend, I offered to come help her for three days to sell her products while she attended the conference. I had no way of knowing that this simple decision to help a friend would completely change my life.

At this time in my life, I was working a corporate job and living an ordinary life. I had greater aspirations for myself but I couldn't seem to get past my fears. Every time I allowed myself to dream about my future, my fears and self doubt would step in to convince me that not only was it not possible, but I wasn't capable. I remained in this holding pattern for approximately eleven years.

I wish I knew then what I know now. How to let go of my fears and just go for it! I had, after all, worked for the "Master of Motivation," Zig Ziglar, early in my career. I had learned from Zig how to set goals and overcome obstacles, but somewhere along the way, I forgot what I learned and gave into the temptation of thinking that happiness and success were for others and not me.

Why is it that so many of us adults give up on our dreams? Why was it so much easier to dream when we were kids? I'm sure you, like me, daydreamed of what you wanted to be when you were growing up. Back then, opportunities seemed endless and our dreams were all within our reach. However, somewhere along the way, many of us lost track of those dreams and the belief that we could do anything worthwhile.

Somewhere deep inside of you, there is still that kid living inside who knows what you really want out of life. It could be writing a book, starting a business, or taking that trip. The problem is, we push those dreams to the back of our minds and minimize the importance of them because they seem too big or too bold. Before long, we forget about them all together.

But, if you just take the time to look within yourself and discover that passion again, you can dust off those dreams and put together a plan to go after them. It's only then that life starts to get exciting. Trust me, I should know.

Since I worked for Zig Ziglar, I knew I loved personal development but I couldn't get my arms around how I could make a living in that area. After all, I wasn't a speaker or an author. In fact, I felt like I had nothing to offer in this area so I continued along the path of just working for a living instead of living to work.

At one point in my life, I got honest with myself and thought about what I really wanted to be, do and have. I kept coming back to speaking, seminars, and impacting peoples' lives just as Zig Ziglar had for so many years. I wouldn't dare admit it to anyone; my real goal was to be like Zig someday. Immediately, I'd catch myself and unconsciously think, "Who do you think you are? How dare you think you could ever measure up and be like Zig Ziglar? Get over yourself and get back to your normal life." And, so I did….until that day I decided to help my friend at her seminar.

I've always been inspired at seminars; being surrounded by other like-minded individuals who share my passion for personal development. That's not very typical of most people and certainly not of my neighbors, my family, or some of my good friends who were surrounding me at that time. But for me, I light up when I'm at a seminar and when I'm around other people who are trying to better themselves. Those who are motivated, and want more for their lives and have goals. I get fired up….and that's exactly what happened to me at this event.

I'm not sure if it was the timing of the seminar or a specific word spoken by one of the speakers, but something shifted in me that day. It was as if someone hit me over the head and I had that "a-ha" moment. For so many years, I'd been saying "Not me! Who am I to do this? I'm no Zig Ziglar!" I'd stop myself in my tracks and put myself down.

But, on this day, I said to myself, *"Why NOT me? I have a unique story to tell. I've gone through some situations that I believe people can relate to. I'm not perfect, but I've learned so much through the years on how to improve myself and I want to share this with people."*

It finally occurred to me that if I had issues with my self-esteem and goal setting even after working for Zig Ziglar all those years, then others may be struggling, too. Maybe there are people who never even heard of goal setting and don't even know where to start. I could help them. So, that's really what prompted me to go and do just that. It was like this light bulb just went off and I have never looked back since.

I really believe that in order to create a happy life, it boils down to belief in yourself. You must believe that you can do something before you can even set out to do it. If you don't have the belief in yourself, you won't be able to accomplish anything. We're all unique; we all have special gifts, we all have a purpose, and I believe it's our job to find that purpose and then live our lives fulfilling it. But, so many of us are held back by these self-limiting beliefs, just like I was. They don't believe they can accomplish their goals, so subconsciously they either sabotage their chance of success, or many just don't even bother trying.

You have to believe in yourself first in order for others to believe in you. People will usually treat you with the same amount of respect as you treat yourself. If you don't have the confidence that you can do a good job, then no one else is going to believe you can do it either. It all starts with you.

So, it took me a long time, but I finally figured out that my passion was to motivate, inspire and encourage others to live happier lives. I made a decision that day to follow my heart and to go after my goal. I literally went home from the seminar and began to write.

Having never written before, I figured I'd have trouble, but the words flew out of me. I had the entire book written in three weeks. For someone who thought I had nothing to say, it was amazing to see how much had been in me for so long, just waiting to come out.

Fast forward. One year later, I'm humbled and proud to say I am a best-selling author, sought after motivational speaker, life mentor, radio host and happier than I've been in my entire life. And, all of this was done while I was still working a full time job. It all started with a decision. It started with me taking a leap of faith and believing in myself.

I'm no different from you. I'm a wife, a mother, a daughter, a sister, just trying to do my best day-in-day-out. I am passionate about life, and I'm passionate about achieving my goals. And, I've had that passion for a long, long time, and I just happen to have followed my dreams, which is why I'm sharing my story with you today.

What about you? What do you really want out of life? What dream do you have that you don't dare tell anyone or believe you can accomplish? If

I can do it, so can you. Don't waste another moment delaying your dreams. Your life is so short and you are given only one chance to make it your best life so why not go for it? If you believe that you can, then I know you will be able to accomplish big goals! I believe in you…and so does that kid deep inside you!

Contact Michelle Prince:
Email: Info@PrincePerformance.com
www.PrincePerformance.com

Bob Burg

Bob Burg is author of the business classic, *Endless Referrals* and co-author (with John David Mann) of the National bestseller, *The Go-Giver* and the recently released, *Go-Givers Sell More.* You may download Chapter One of either book by visiting www.Burg.com.

Contact Bob Burg:
www.Burg.com

Visionary Thinking … Within a System
by Bob Burg

The very title of this article would seem to be contrarian, wouldn't it? After all, how could one even attempt to be visionary (that is, an innovative and forward-looking thinker) within an already-established system?

First, it's important to understand what I mean by a "system" so that we are coming at this from the same perspective.

I define a "system" as: "The process of predictably achieving a goal based on a logical and specific set of how-to principles."

The key to a successful system is that word predictability. In other words, if it's been proven that by doing A you'll get the desired results of B then you know that all you need to do is A and continue to do A and eventually you'll get the results you want: B.

Of course, there is nothing especially visionary in this definition; you're simply following something that has already been created.

On the other hand, creativity – which is often a trait of a visionary – is itself something that typically builds upon information that is already out there in the ether. A substantial amount of research has shown that even those who seem to come up with new and ingenious ideas practically out of nowhere, have had many years of training and experience within a particular paradigm or model that has provided them sufficient knowledge to create or envision this "new thing."

I am not your typical visionary. I tend not to be the creative type. I'm not even an early adopter of those things others create. (I mean, in the mid-nineties, I actually made the brilliant prediction that, "this Internet thing will never take hold and become anything big!")

However, if we can include creating a particular type of business brand within a system as being visionary, then I at least semi-qualify.

Here's what I mean:

From the moment I stepped out of my two previous fields, television broadcasting and direct sales, in order to become a professional speaker, I recognized a challenge I would have: there are a ton of people who already do what I do. And not only do they do what I do, they know pretty much all that I know … if not more.

Now, following a system, I knew I'd be able to build a profitable speaking business because, well, that's what systems do: they help you accomplish whatever you set out to do. However, I knew that the system alone would do very little to separate me from the rest of the many other highly-qualified and excellent speakers with whom I'd eventually compete for corporate and organizational seminars.

Here's where "envisioning within a system" comes in.

I took what was already out there—the system for building a speaking practice and the information I could share that would be of value to conference attendees – and married it with a unique strength of mine.

My unique strength is that ... I'm a very slow learner!

"What?" you might ask "how is that a strength?"

Because it made me much more sensitive to those who were as slow a learner as I am. And, I knew that if I could teach in such a way that the slowest of the slow could learn my information and apply it immediately (and teaching for immediate application happens to be a strength of mine), then so would everyone else who was not nearly as slow a learner as those attendees and me.

Soon, word began to get around that when you attended a Bob Burg seminar, not only would you get a reasonably funny, entertaining, and hard-hitting talk with valuable information (which you could get from many, many, many other speakers just as well) but also that, regardless of where you were on the learning curve, you could take that information and apply it with confidence in the real world of sales *the very next day* and attain significant and immediate results.

This gave me a competitive edge that has served me (and hopefully my clients) for years. This is not to take anything away from my very worthy fellow speakers who also speak on my topic; it's just one thing extra I bring to the table that helps me position myself as being of value to the client.

Let's look at one other area in which I was able to envision within an already formed structure (i.e. a system).

Lately, over perhaps the past fifteen years or so, there has emerged what seems to me a strange phenomenon in the media: the loud-mouthed know-it-all who has built up a raving fan base *because of* (not *in spite of*) their arrogant and condescending persona. I won't name names; several probably come to mind. I also know some speakers who have taken on this kind of persona and, while it pains me to say it, have not only done well with it, but are actually adored by many.

Oh well, life is life. We can try and find the reasons for things like that but, when it comes right down to it, *it is what it is*. (And, yes, perhaps the Hokey-Pokey indeed *is* what it's all about.)

While this doesn't mean we need be like them (in fact, I'd hope we are not) we can absolutely look at the situation and use it to find our own distinctive and marketable voice; again, be that *creative visionary* within an already existing framework or system. Obviously, I'm coming at this from the viewpoint of a speaker, and will use myself once again as an example, but you can apply it to your field, whatever that may be.

Like some of those "contrarian curmudgeons" I am indeed "contrarian." I often take a different route when I feel it serves best. For example, I speak on the topic of Business Networking, yet I put *very* little importance on the practice of using business cards. Indeed, I suggest to my readers and live audiences that you not even *offer* your card until and unless you are specifically asked for it. Without going into an explanation right now as to why, let's just say that I am most likely the only speaker on my topic to make that suggestion. That is being contrarian.

This does not conflict with following a system; it means that having learned a system thoroughly, I am then able to know how and when to veer from it without getting into trouble.

Again, I am a contrarian. But – and this is key – I'm not a curmudgeon. I'm actually (hmm, how do I say this?) "nice." Yes, I said it … I'm a nice guy (proving, of course, that *nice guys actually do finish first*). I don't enjoy insulting people but rather enjoy making people feel good about themselves. While I'll always defend a particular position when principle is involved, I'll also always do my best to be polite and kind to the person with whom I disagree.

What I've done – via articles, interviews, published books, blogs, etc. – is to position myself as *contrarian, but not curmudgeon,* as a speaker and author who often does and says things differently from the rest and in such a way as to provide significant value, but in a manner that people were always made to feel they were safe and in conversation with someone who truly cared about *them*, not just himself.

The big lesson here is this: If (like me) you don't think of yourself as "a visionary," that is no reason to think you cannot do new and creative things and effectively position yourself as someone or something special in your market. In other words, to be a visionary, you don't necessarily have to be "creative." You only need be able to look at what has already been done by others and then find your uniqueness, your true authentic self … and communicate it.

Contact Bob Burg:
www.Burg.com

Laura Newman

Laura Newman lives her passion by showing individuals and businesses how to express and share their joy and appreciation easily, inexpensively and while having fun through her SendOutCards business. She also created *"Yoga Lite, Exercise To Go,"* a completely audio CD so people can do simple stretching, balancing and meditation exercises conveniently, any place and any time, to feel great. As a professional entertainer (Shamrock the Clown), speaker and writer, Laura shares her joyful philosophy of finding fun living in the moment!

Contact Laura Newman:

www.sendoutcards.com/lauranewman
www.yogalite.Info
www.laughoutloud.Biz
shamrocknew@hotmail.com
954-580-7262
Facebook: Laura Newman
Twitter: Ljnewman
Linkedin: Laura J Newman

Laugh Out Loud
by Laura Newman

A friend once asked me if I laugh even while making love. I assured him I often do, as I do in pretty much every situation. If there is a quirk in something, I'll find the humor in it. There is love in laughter. There is comfort in laughter. There is success in laughter. There is even a saying, "Funny is money."

At the midlife crisis age of forty-five, I started looking for that one deal, that one secret (why is everything such a secret lately?), that one amazing product that I could order from late night TV for only six easy payments of $500 each if I ordered before midnight, that would catapult me to "real" success. I found a deal in real estate. I watched a video. I ordered (a few) products. And I came full circle back to me; trusting my own instincts, defining my own success and joy, which for me was not found in a McMansion, or a Rolls Royce, or on a private island. (I enjoy those things; they just don't define happiness for me!)

In my quest for success, as I allowed others to define it, I got a bit lost until I finally realized my own secret to success is simple. I found it by thinking about how I define happiness, and remembering how I found it the last time I lost it. So, I started my journey anew (as we do every single moment anyway) and along our path, I re-discovered even more secrets as if for the first time.

Secret #1: If it's not fun, stop doing it. This may sound completely hedonistic. It is. Life is too short to spend its precious moments doing things that make you want to complain, moan (not in a good way) and generally be a drag to be with. A corollary to this is knowing that it is possible to find some tiny element of fun in what you are doing until you can stop. Think about how. You may have to think really, really hard. Maybe it's second hand fun (being the youngest of twelve children I know all about second hand stuff) like remembering the fun you'll have eating the dinner that was paid for by doing what you are doing. Find the silver lining.

Secret #2: Keep moving toward doing that which you believe will be enjoyable. Create a dream board with pictures and encouraging words to help you visualize what gives you joy. "Virtualize" your dream, as suggested by Mark Victor Hanson and Robert Allen in their book, *Cash in a Flash*. Make it as real as possible by imagining it with all your senses. See it. Touch it. Smell it. Hear it. Taste it. Mark and Bob even write press releases about the books they haven't yet written being on the New York Times bestseller list. Wayne Dyer mocks up the covers of books he is contemplating writing. If it works for these amazingly successful, intelligent people that's good enough for me.

Secret #3: If what you thought would be that one great deal or product or business opportunity turns out not to be, admit it. Figure out how to stop the bleeding, and move on to something else that doesn't hurt.

Secret #4: If what you are doing is not helping anyone but yourself, or is hurting others either outright or by neglect, stop it. Figure out a way to make it beneficial for at least one other person. Or dog.

Secret #5: If all else fails, apply bumper sticker wisdom. "I tried to contain myself, but I escaped" sums up my life philosophy very succinctly. "Commit random acts of kindness" is another favorite.

Identifying your vision is sometimes the most challenging step in living it. Or, perhaps the most challenging step for some is allowing your passion to be big enough to get you through the rough spots of fulfilling your vision.

Getting clear on your vision itself, the passion that drives your vision is a good starting point. For example, my vision is a world of family, friends and even people I don't know tapping into their own joy; expressing their joy fully, and sharing their joy virally. My passion is connecting with people, talking with them, learning about them, sharing laughter with them. I know when I draw on the joy within myself, other people can feel it. I believe we all have abundant joy within. Too often I do not see people expressing even a little of their joy.

My "Aha" moment was realizing that my passion is not so much about spreading joy (that is, thinking I can give someone else joy), as it is about helping others recognize and release the joy already within themselves.

When we live our passion, and believe we are on purpose in our vision, we are usually having fun. When we are having fun, we do better at whatever it is we are doing. And then, it cycles back; the fact that what we did we did well, and were passionate about it, makes it even more fun. (Just reading those three sentences was fun, wasn't it?!) When we teach ourselves the value of enjoying the moment of enjoying each step in creating our vision, we are making the process itself part of the reward of creating our vision.

To me, joy is a fundamental component of success.

Mark Twain says, "Twenty years from now, you will be more disappointed by the things you didn't do than by the ones you did. So throw off the bowlines, sail away from the safe harbor. Catch the trade winds in your sails. Explore. Dream. Discover."

Once you identify your vision and make it real in your own mind, there are certain character traits you may want to cultivate to help you bring your vision to life:

- **Decisive desire.**
- **Willingness to do whatever it takes.**
- **Creative thinking.**
- **Determination and persistence to do whatever it takes.**
- **Belief and confidence that you can make your vision come alive.**

Do you truly want to make your vision your reality? Sometimes you think you want something, only to realize later, we really didn't want it. Maybe someone else thought we should want it and you let them convince you it was what you wanted. Maybe what you thought you wanted turned out to be not quite what you thought it would be. Sometimes just giving a little more thought to what you think you want spares you some expensive, hard-learned lessons. And then, sometimes we just have to do certain things to find out they are not what we want! **Do you have the willingness to do whatever it takes to fulfill your vision?** I once thought about running for public office, but realized I was not willing at that time to commit to the time required, the travel, and the constant scrutiny. Think about the known tradeoffs. Don't be discouraged by them, just make yourself aware of them.

Have you done anything to develop your creative thinking more? The cliché, "Think outside the box" (more bumper sticker wisdom!) is helpful when you are pursuing your desire. I have a friend who was agoraphobic. She did not leave her house for several years because she was fearful. She loved clowns, and decided perhaps if she could train herself to be a clown, and dress not as herself but as her alter-ego clown, that might help her overcome her fear of leaving her house. It worked. That's thinking creatively outside the box.

Do you have enough determination and persistence to continue what you start? Some of us are more prone to throwing in the towel when we face challenges in even fairly inconsequential undertakings. Persistence is a habit you can cultivate daily that will serve us well throughout life.

Do you have the belief in yourself that you can create your dream, your vision? There is much psychology I know nothing about that might explain why some of us lack self-confidence. The only way I know of to overcome self-doubt is, recognize you attempted to do something and you "failed"; we can reframe our "failure" as a learning experience. When we learn from our "failures," we turn them into successful lessons.

The only real failure is in not even going for what we want. If it doesn't work out exactly the way we anticipate, so be it. Use your creative thinking to figure out a different way. Meantime, you've now developed a new way of thinking, and strengthened your confidence. These conventional techniques are the secrets that help many people achieve their vision, and I use them. The "secret" technique I find most helpful, though, is finding joy in everything I do.

And laughing. Out loud. Often.

Contact Laura Newman:
www.sendoutcards.com/lauranewman
www.yogalite.Info
www.laughoutloud.Biz
shamrocknew@hotmail.com
954-580-7262
Facebook: Laura Newman
Twitter: Ljnewman
Linkedin: Laura J Newman

Fran Asaro

Fran Asaro is the President and founder of Thrive Any Way Personal and Business Coaching. Fran created her "Life By Design" program to assist those looking to discover their natural life rhythm. With undaunted commitment and compassion, Fran is an intuitive and innovative thinker, who provides a gentle approach for those seeking guidance, increased selfesteem and greater empowerment.

Fran's "Life By Design" program is an individual process to unfold full self expression. After years of making her mark as a successful business owner and top-producing Real Estate Professional, Fran is passionate about her greatest purpose; helping others find their authentic life path.

In addition to her business, Fran volunteers as a self-esteem coach for victims of domestic violence.

Contact Fran Asaro:
www.ThriveAnyway.com
Fran@ThriveAnyway.com
(954) 370-8001

Life by Design: Thriving on YOUR Terms
by Fran Asaro

W ho's been sleeping in YOUR bed? This is a good question for those living someone else's idea of life. Are any of the following life patterns familiar to yours?

The Perpetual Student

Stacey woke one day to her regular routine, reading daily affirmations and excerpts from a meditation book. She listened to a motivational CD in her car while driving to work and envisioned the new life she will create for herself. She goes to her networking meetings and interacts with colleagues, in hope of connecting with that 'right' person who will help make a difference in her life. She signs up for a 3-day workshop which promises to deliver success, freedom, or enlightenment.

She notices that all around her, there are people truly 'getting' the message. In her world, there are those who are actually living the life they love by applying all of these practices, but Stacey is different. Every time she embraces a particular technique, she is left still feeling empty. Is there something wrong? Is she not worthy of a more fulfilled life? How much more time and energy will it take to achieve bliss?

The Intimidated

John wakes every day to his usual routine breakfast, work and home again with intermittent social engagements. He notices his friends are all "up to" something in their life, such as opening new businesses or creating new projects and each one appears to be involved in major life activities. John feels intimidated. He doesn't have those aspirations. Maybe he does, but he cannot launch himself amidst the same level of greatness that his friends seem to emit. His low self-esteem has kept him from massaging his own ideas and creativity and he simply doesn't know how to move forward, so John continues his life -- as is.

The Fearful Flyer

Alexis is a corporate employee, working with the same company for 20 years. She goes to work every day performing to the best of her ability. As time goes on, Alexis has a yearning to quit her job and to feel more open in her self-expression. Her friends and family insist that she should be grateful simply to have a job. They project their personal fears, which inhibits her dream of entrepreneurship. She has a sense that she is dying a slow death yet she cannot take the leap necessary without someone who can align with her vision.

The Daring Designer

Robert is a retail manager who goes to work following the structure of the company and his life is just "okay." He has had an ardent desire to be and to have more. He has a long history of studying personal development and researching new adventures to participate in. One day, Robert decides it's time to gather the information he's learned over the years and to finally take action, and after some preparation, feels ready to jump in.

Robert creates a new business that exhilarates him and challenges every fiber of his being. His family and friends share their concerns with him about the poor economy, lack and limitations, downfalls and the probability of failure. But he goes forth anyway. He sees others with much more experience performing greater feats than his and still, he goes forth anyway. He stays true to his objective - to live life on HIS terms! Yes, he is pitted against finances, rejection, hurdles along with doubts and fears, but he stays true. He knows he needs support. He chooses someone to stand at his finish line for him to encourage him along the way, to see nothing less than his ultimate success. He enjoys the entire experience because for the first time in his life it is HIS experience. Right, wrong, success, failure, it's his and he would rather fail at his life than succeed at someone else's.

Own Your Own

There are many scenarios of those who sacrifice having a life they love. Whether it be due to a handicap, an addiction, or history of oppression, there is still a place in this life for all of us to THRIVE.

If you aren't loving your life, chances are you are living someone else's idea for your life and that's what feels uncomfortable. If this conversation seems unsettling, then maybe it's time for you to begin creating your OWN path and do life on YOUR terms – and at your OWN pace.

Free from Oppression

Coming from an oppressive upbringing, it took me years to begin listening to my own guidance system and building not only an authentic life, but a life I truly LOVE.

I grew up on Long Island, New York, raised Italian, Catholic. With a dominant father who preferred to tell me what to think as opposed to finding out whom I truly was, I went for many years feeling like two people: the person I was "groomed" to be, and the passionate person I truly am. I always felt there was more for me. What it was I didn't know, but I pursued many avenues of development and embraced the process of finding out.

I knew I was seeking a life of fun and freedom but struggled to unleash my old patterns. The more I went to others to teach me, the more it was reinforced that someone else's way was better than mine. As a result, I didn't soar from all the learning I was engaged in. I became more frustrated by my lack of progression and it did a lot to impede my growth, self-esteem and empowerment. Eventually I realized I had to break away from the beliefs of others and begin my OWN quest for finding 'ME'. I began doing introspective work and chose to surround myself with people who would support me in my natural way of being.

I gave up a long successful career as a Realtor to become a Life Coach, which is what I consider to be my life's work. Now I design my own schedule, food plan, exercise regimen or whatever I may need on my journey. Some of it flows and some is a process, but it's mine just the same. I feel happy and satisfied that I am following my own "true north" and not someone else's.

I bump up against adversity every day and yet find myself smiling, or crying tears of joy now that I have found my own life rhythm. It's possible at any age and in any situation and we all deserve to thrive in life. REALLY!

I am now committed to helping others "thrive" in living life on their terms, helping them tap into their individuality and connecting them to their right to have it. It's a gentle, loving approach to joy. This is not for the faint of heart. It is however for those seeking more for themselves. Below are a few philosophies of "Life by Design." It begins here and goes with you everywhere.

Fits Like a Glove

Having a life that fits like a glove is a life where you fully own what you are doing and were meant to do, where one thoroughly enjoys the process as well as the outcome, where one feels comfortable and warm.

Challenging the 'Experts'

There are many amazing teachers in the world including speakers, authors, and leaders. They all have a message to deliver and many of them have a process that worked for them and they lovingly want to share to make a difference.

While one or many of the teachers' lessons may resonate with you, there arc those who feel a pull towards something more or different. This is further evidence that it's okay to challenge the experts. This is where "Life by Design" can be invaluable.

We are ALL standing on the shoulders of someone else's greatness and this energetic pull you have could mean it's YOUR turn to create anew. Listen to your inner dialog for this and respond.

Quenching your Inner Thirst for an Authentic Life

Maybe you have a calling, or maybe you have an idea of how you want your life to be. Many of us have a mission that we just have to complete and we don't know what it is or how to accomplish it. The first thing to do is to honor that thirst for more. You have a purpose and it will manifest once you tap into the awareness that you do. The rest will be a natural process to unfold.

Dancing to the Rhythm you were Born With

You may have a lifelong awareness that there is more for you in life. That's great. But even if you don't, there is a message you camc here to deliver. There is a "dance" that is authentically yours. All that needs to be done is to awaken your rhythm and begin.

Creating from Nothing

You get to create from nothing. Consider the bushwhacker in the jungle who holds the machete, cuts through the brush and creates the path for others. It's scary, unfamiliar and it's downright uncomfortable. But if it were comfortable, most likely it would be someone else's path. So be the first one to create this path. Create from nothing.

Reinvent that wheel.

Rock that boat.

Claim your mark on the world.

Contact Fran Asaro:

www.ThriveAnyway.com
Fran@ThriveAnyway.com
(954) 370-8001

Chapter 2

SETTING YOURSELF FREE: OVERCOMING FEARS AND LIMITING BELIEFS

"Too many of us are not living our dreams
because we are living our fears."
~ Les Brown

Introduction
by Nancy Matthews

Our minds are "Folk Tale Factories", constantly making up stories, stories that create our belief system, our programming and subsequently our actions and our lives. The problem more often than not, is that these stories about our past, what happened, how others felt about us and how we feel about ourselves are not necessarily true stories. Have you ever been stuck or stopped from achieving a goal? Have you noticed behavior patterns that result in sabotaging your goals and dreams? The roots can likely be found in underlying programs and limiting beliefs. The stories we have been telling ourselves for years such as, I'm not good enough, fear of criticism and failure, money is the root of all evil, and so many other stories that don't serve our highest and best. Living as a "Visionary with Guts" gives you the opportunity to put your "Folk Tale Factory" to good use and create stories that do serve you. Stories that support you in living the life of your dreams. You are good enough, you deserve health, wealth and happiness and it's yours for the asking.

Is fear likely to show up? Absolutely! Are there times when you will (temporarily) fail? Absolutely! A "Visionary with Guts" expects fear and failure to show up. The true measure of success is how you respond when fear and failure show up. When fear shows up we say "Thanks for coming, I was expecting you. Now get out of my way, I've got dreams to live!"

I have learned to live in faith instead of fear. When we live our lives in fear, we experience stress, worry and anxiety. When we live our lives in faith we experience hope, excitement and positive expectation. Which would you prefer?

Susan Somerset Webb

Susan Somerset Webb, EFT-ADV, endured an undiagnosed illness for more than a year, when she was introduced to EFT as a last resort. Little did she know that it was the key to restoring her emotional and physical health.

Inspired by her return to health, Susan became a dedicated Energy Psychology practitioner, helping hundreds of people nationally and internationally through her popular workshops, as well as her busy private practice. Clients have experienced relief from issues as varied as trauma, pain, stress, depression, anxiety and OCD, and report making great strides in both their professional and personal lives.

Susan is an intuitive workshop facilitator, success coach, and well-known speaker and corporate trainer. She uses powerful tools such as EFT, TAT, Psych K, Energy Medicine and Matrix Energetics to help her clients reprogram their subconscious beliefs in far less time than most other therapeutic modalities.

Contact Susan Somerset Webb:
www.TapIntoYourLife.com

Powerful Beyond Measure
by Susan Somerset-Webb

"Our deepest fear is not that we are inadequate.
Our deepest fear is that we are powerful beyond measure."
Marianne Williamson

It was 1994 when this quote first brought me to tears. Not just tears. Gut wrenching sobs at the time, and every time I read it. What was it about this statement that kept me from maintaining my well-established composure? It was the fundamental truth of this compelling statement. It was the first time I became aware that I had lived my life in fear.

Did my life irrevocably change at that moment? If it did, the change wasn't noticeable and it was nothing compared to the way my life would be altered in the coming years.

Life has a way of getting our attention. It might be a whisper at first, then a little tap on the shoulder. If we aren't paying any attention, it might be a frisky shove. Still taking no notice? Then it's time for the big guns. It can come in any form and none of it is expected, or, for that matter, pleasant. But whatever shows up, it causes you to stop and examine what you've been creating. Caroline Myss calls it your "desert experience."

I created my desert experience in 2001 shortly after 9/11. I didn't know anyone personally who had lost a loved one in that terrible tragedy but I felt impacted by it in a way that I had no words for. I now know that it had an enormous energetic effect not just on me, but the entire world. I just didn't understand what it meant at the time.

Combine 9/11 with another life-altering experience later on in that year, and bingo; I had my desert experience. It came in the form of an undiagnosed illness which kept me in bed and unable to work for nearly a year. During most of that year, I did very little but focus on what a bad hand I had been dealt and various ways to end my life. I lost everything - my house, my savings. I was fifty-two years-old. I thought my life was over.

Then I got a call from a friend who said she had taken a workshop in Miami and that "there were miracles happening" in the meeting room. She said, "I bet if you learned the technique, it might help you." That technique was EFT (Emotional Freedom Techniques), and the workshop was given by Gary Craig, its founder. My friend was right. Not only did learning EFT help me, it saved my life.

Flash forward to 2010. My health is better than it's been in many years, I am at complete peace, I'm now an Advanced EFT Practitioner and have helped hundreds of people transform their lives with this and other amazing Energy Psychology techniques. My life feels like a miracle.

So, would you be interested in experiencing a similar shift? I'm going to warn you right upfront – a transformation like this involves facing one of the biggest unconscious fears every human heart harbors: that you are powerful beyond measure. And that the suffering in your life is because you have not been able to correctly harness that power.

The unconscious is a vast and mysterious territory, which consumes and expends large amounts of physical and emotional energy. This energy expenditure serves to maintain our beliefs, our drives, our behaviors and to preserve our sense of security and safety. For the purpose of survival and energy efficiency, the unconscious is a quick study. Lessons are learned the first time. But here's the catch. Once a belief is set in place, it is very hard to identify and reprogram it as new information might necessitate.

Fear beliefs are among the most quickly learned and difficult to unlearn. Many people chip away at their fears, heroically pushing themselves through private battles to reach victory. No one can doubt the value of the insights we get access to in workshops, seminars, and books. There are, however, some of us, who no matter how hard we try, find it difficult, if not impossible, to push through our fears. We struggle to change the behaviors of overreacting, blaming, etc. Some of us need another kind of help to change the way we see ourselves and others.

Our hearts threaten to fight to the death to hold onto habits and beliefs. However irrelevant in the present, they were first established to create a sense of safety. Some of us need a way - a back door of sorts - to access and change those beliefs without dismantling the sense of safety they were designed to preserve. EFT, according to many cutting-edge researchers and scientists, is that back door.

EFT is easy to learn, and simple to do. It's not hocus-pocus. It doesn't involve hundreds of hours of therapy or dredging up emotionally devastating landmines from your past. In fact, it's a tool you can learn in just minutes – and use for a lifetime. In using EFT, you access your body's energy system (meridians), just as you would do in acupuncture.

However, instead of needles, you'll use your fingertips to tap gently on nine points on your head and body. Very simple.

But first, back to the beginning. At birth, we are hard-wired with only two fears: falling and loud noises. We acquire all other fears along the way, mostly before we reach age six, and mostly in response to non-physical threats. All acquired fears are a compilation of beliefs we adopt from the people around us in an attempt to ensure our survival. Fear evokes one of three responses each time the emotion arises - fight, flight or freeze. When the perceived threat is not physical, our response is often to freeze. Rather than living an inspired and exhilarating life of peace and purpose, the obvious outcome is a life immobilized by stuck habits and fearful beliefs.

EFT is a process of combining a running dialogue with tapping on strategic points on your body to access your stored fears and release them. While you may not be aware of the fears you carry with you, those fears may show up in your life as pain, illness, addictions, depression, anxiety, eating disorders, obsessive-compulsive disorders, and challenges in your performance and relationships at work and at home.

For almost a decade, using EFT in my own life and my private practice, I've witnessed what can only be described as miracles. Clients, even if they are initially skeptical, have used this technique to release their fear and embrace their own power. The results? From their own Western medical professionals, they hear words like: "unexpected recovery," "impressive turnaround," and, "Whatever it is that you're doing, keep doing." It makes sense when you think about it. Even these Western doctors agree that 80-85% of all illness is created by stress.

Why am I telling you all this? I sit across from people every day who are depressed, anxiety-ridden, suicidal, and facing challenges they never wished for or expected. I tell them what I want you to know: You ARE powerful beyond measure. The power to live the life you desire is at your fingertips.

EFT is just one of a host of powerful Energy Psychology techniques available today. Dr. David Feinstein, renowned author of *The Promise of Energy Psychology,* shared this with me recently about this burgeoning field, "I wake up every morning and say, 'This is a miracle.' "

I want to share this miracle with you, if you are interested in learning more about how to stop the fear and create a more powerful life. Visit me online at www.TapIntoYourLife.com for a video demonstration of this technique, a diagram of the tapping points you'll use, client testimonials, and information on workshops, classes, and private sessions (in person and on the phone).

The rest of the quote I began with illustrates the importance of transforming our fears. I hope you'll join me in this movement toward empowered living:

> *"...It is our light, not our darkness, that most frightens us. We ask ourselves, 'Who am I to be brilliant, gorgeous, talented, and fabulous?' Actually, who are you not to be? You are a child of God. Your playing small doesn't serve the world. There's nothing enlightened about shrinking so that other people won't feel insecure around you. We are all meant to shine, as children do. We are born to make manifest the glory of God that is within us. It's not just in some of us, it's in everyone. And as we let our own light shine, we unconsciously give other people permission to do the same. As we are liberated from our own fear, our presence automatically liberates others."*
> *--Marianne Williamson*

Contact Susan Somerset Webb:

www.TapIntoYourLife.com

Samantha Roose

Samantha Roose lives in Williamsburg, Virginia, where she serves with her family, in the ministry of Fort Roose. She is a junior in high school and is homeschooled along with her ten siblings. Not only a tri-athlete, author, and musician, she competes on a speech and debate team and leads a bible study for young women. Samantha loves worshiping God through dance and enjoys the opportunity to impart this passion to younger students as a dance instructor. She has been able to encourage other young women around her to know the truth and pursue their visions.

Contact Samantha Roose:

Samantha@NoGreaterWealth.com

F.E.A.R.
False Evidence Appearing Real
by Samantha Roose

The battle is all around us. The enemy is relentless. No one is exempt from the fight. F.E.A.R., False Evidence Appearing Real, is a real enemy fought on the battlefield of the mind.

My comrades and I are driven by a vision—a vision of freedom. Fear has held many of us captive, preventing us from achieving our goals, plaguing us with false evidence dictating our lives. Now, no matter how grueling the combat, my comrades and I are willing to fight. If we do not, we will never be free to reach our vision.

While waiting for the scouts bearing news of our enemy's position, I girded myself with the belt of truth.

Pacing before us, our general reiterated the words of our captains, Timothy, John, Paul and many others, "Three hundred sixty-five times I have commanded you, do not be afraid. That's once for every day of the year. Furthermore, I have not given you the spirit of fear but of power and of love and of a sound mind. Know the truth and the truth will set you free. For this battle is not against the human abilities of this world, but against authorities and spiritual forces. Fear is merely our enemy's weapon. Our adversary, the Master of masquerade, has disguised his weapons as fear lies, which he puts in your minds as thoughts. Fear is the feeling of these thoughts—the wound of the weapon. This battle is a clash of conflicting wills, yours and his; your only weapon is the truth, which is in you. The battlefield is your mind. Fear not!"

The heavy morning fog still hung heavy with the general's words when the scouts returned. After some time the general resumed his position before the ranks.

"The scouts have succeeded in bringing us valuable information about our opponents' tactics and positions," he began. "Our enemy is divided into three forces. Each section will attempt to destroy us from a different position. One will attack by telling you that you 'lack resources' filling your mind with thoughts such as, 'I don't have enough ammunition'. 'There is not enough time...' Another will assail you with the fear of 'not being good enough,' through thoughts telling you that you do not have what it takes, that someone can do it better than you can, or that you're not good enough. And, the third will assault you with memories of your past failures. But, take courage. These assaults are merely thoughts. The way you choose to combat these thoughts of false evidence will determine the outcome of this war. As our comrade Orison Swett Marden has reminded us, 'Most of our obstacles will melt away if, instead of cowering before them, we would make up our minds to walk boldly through them.'

Before he had time to continue, a sentry flushed and panting, reported hoarsely, "Sir, the enemy is advancing."

Immediately, the regiments were dispatched.

"Remember," the general's voice rose above the noise, "your actions will always follow your thoughts…" The rest of his words were lost in the commotion.

Engaged in fierce combat my mind echoed with the general's words: "Fear not! Fear is the feeling of your thoughts." A grenade exploded somewhere nearby jerking me back to reality. As I crouched down to reload, I heard myself say, "We don't have enough ammunition to finish the battle." Then I realized I had fallen into the enemies' trap of 'our general had not provided what we needed for battle.' I repelled the false evidence by turning to the truth, 'there *is* enough ammunition.'

We don't have the facilities to take care of the wounded, I thought as I watched a friend crumple to the ground and lie motionless. "No," I shook my head in exasperation. "That's not true! We do have enough ammunition; and we have the highest level of care available." It was then that I realized what the general had meant by, 'Your mind is your battlefield…you cannot win this battle with weapons.' We were definitely being attacked with thoughts, which, if accepted, defeated us dissipating our dreams. Suddenly, it dawned on me; the *truth* is my weapon.

Many have gone before us in this battle with truth as their weapon, I thought. Mother Theresa reached her goal by focusing on the truth, I reasoned. She was a nun, whom God chose to care for the "poorest of the poor." Ignoring her lack of resources, she focused on what she *had* to accomplish her vision. Because she refused fear when it attempted to extinguish her vision she was able to reach millions of people, accomplishing the goal God had for her. Why could not I do the same?

Still fighting for our vision, my unit transferred to a defensive position. While on guard, I continually thought of what I didn't know about war. I couldn't stop thinking about how much better everyone else was at firing the artillery than I, and how much stronger and experienced they were. Believing these lies paralyzed me, rendering me unable to operate the artillery. And then, I remembered the general's words: Your actions will always follow your thoughts." *Just more of the enemies lies*, I told myself, and fought on.

Returning to my tent, after I was relieved from sentry duty, my mind again, returned to my thoughts. Opening my journal, my eyes fell on an entry entitled *Fear*. Memories washed over me as I read:

"God has continued to guide my dancing career as I instruct others in dance. Unfortunately, fear almost stole my opportunity to assist in coordinating our program's dress rehearsal because I compared my dancing abilities to my friends' talents, who have been dancing all their lives. But, when I chose to focus on the gifts I had been given instead of comparing my abilities to my friends', I was able to conquer fear and help coordinate a successful and orderly rehearsal."

Written in the margins I found a quote by Brendan Francis, "Many of our fears are tissue paper-thin, and a single courageous step would carry us through them."

My fear had been, that in comparing myself to others I would not measure up, I mused. *My single courageous step, which overcame my fear had been recognizing the truth and believing it. The battle had been fought and won in my mind! And once again, my weapon had been the girdle of truth.*

After my regiment replaced the 32nd division on the frontlines, I was assaulted, yet again, on the battlefield of my mind. It seemed as if I could never get away from this enemy, called Fear. Memories breathed down my neck reminding me of all my past failed attempts. I wondered, "Is this how Roy Riegels felt that unforgettable night in 1929?" I rehearsed the incident in my mind.

Sometime during the first half of the 1929 Rose Bowl between Georgia Tech and the University of California, Riegles became confused and started running the ball in the wrong direction. Halftime came and the men collected in the locker room. If you've ever played football, you know that a coach usually has a great deal to say to his team during halftime. This time Coach Price was silent.

The announcement came—three minutes before the second half. "Men," Coach Price said clearing his throat, "the same team that played the first half will start the second." Everyone got up and headed out, all but Riegles.

"Roy," the coach called, "did you hear me? The same team that played the first half will start the second."

"Coach," Riegles looked up with tear-stained cheeks, "I can't do it to save my life. I've ruined the University of California. I've ruined myself. I couldn't face that crowd in the stadium to save my life."

Placing his hand on Riegles' shoulder Coach Price said, "Roy, get up and go back, the game is only half over!" Roy did return to the game with enthusiasm and no one has ever played inspired football as he did that second half.

Another courageous warrior, Winston Churchill once said, "Courage is going from failure to failure without losing enthusiasm."

Enthusiastically, I resolved to reject the horrors of my past failures and return to the battlefield. After all, the war is only half over.

Gradually the deafening sound of war dwindled and died away. Smiles illuminated the weary faces of the soldiers up and down the lines as they realized what was happening. Cheers erupted breaking the serene silence.

"Freedom from Fear," men shouted as they burst from their trenches.

The whole war seemed to fade away as if it had been a nightmare. Dreams and visions for the future were freely exchanged. Hopes and desires were voiced. Fear no longer shackled any individual. We had fought for freedom and won the battlefield of our minds.

As I walked through the camp, individuals I didn't recognize approached me telling me how they were impacted by my fight against fear.

"Hey, I just wanted you to know that I wouldn't have been able to keep fighting if I hadn't heard you repeating the truth," said one enthusiastic fighter. "Billy Graham was right when he said: 'Courage is contagious. When a brave man takes a stand, the spines of others are stiffened'—you sure stiffened mine!"

A young visionary stopped me not long after, "You are the bravest sight I have ever seen. Thank you for your inspiration." Then quoting Lucius Annaeus Seneca he said, "The bravest sight in the world is to see a great man struggling against adversity."

As I entered my tent, yet another man ran up to me. He placed a note in my hand on which were written the words of a Japanese proverb, "Fear is only as deep as the mind allows."

Through those words of encouragement, I realized that my decision to speak truth to myself had affected others as well. I had commanded the battlefield of my mind and attained victory over the real enemy, Fear, in a real battle common to every man. Fear no longer held me in bondage keeping me from moving forward toward my vision. Finally, I was confident that I could achieve my goals. Returning to a new routine of life—fighting fear and pursuing my visions, the words of my general echoed in my mind, "…I have not given you a spirit of fear…know the truth and the truth will set you free…your actions will always follow your thoughts…this battle will begin and end in a thought…fear not…" At that moment, I resolved to continue the fight against **F**alse **E**vidence which **A**ppears **R**eal. As I march forth from the thick of battle, I enthusiastically fight for my vision.

Contact Samantha Roose:

Samantha@NoGreaterWealth.com

Felice Cellini

Felice calls gratitude her attitude for living in the moment, that fantastic time zone for realizing opportunity. Facing forward and bringing joyous expectancy with her, she shares with others a contagious sense of optimism.

She also shares openly the challenges of living fully through fears and grief: the loss of a child and the overcoming of addiction.

She loves being a mom involved, considers it an honor to care for many as a Physician Assistant, and is grateful for the blessing of being in recovery.

Felice is known for smiling often while ever reminding others of the miracles ahead.

Contact Felice Cellini:
felicecellini@hotmail.com

FEAR:
A Choice We Need Not Make
by Felice Cellini

Some time ago, I attended a weekend event. One of those jam-packed with new adventures and shared insight. It was during this weekend that I realized a simple truth about fear.

It was a midafternoon Saturday. The room was filled to capacity with approximately 1,000 people of different backgrounds and similar interests, one more eager than the other to master the dynamics behind prosperity and growth. Each participant, willing to do whatever it took to venture forward in our endeavor.

As one of the many exercises to expand our understanding of ourselves, we were all told to stand and line up in rows. That we would be called up to the stage in groups and would be taught how to become "fire-eaters." The mood in the room changed instantly and without much thought, the crowd was separated into people who were eager and excited to conquer this new challenge, and those who were petrified to even think about trying.

I, being one of the excited folks, was chatting with all those around me, dancing to the music playing; hoping beyond hope I would be one of the photographed "fire-eaters" so I could share the experience with my kids when I returned home. I was giddy and had a difficult time waiting in line. I was so "psyched" to get up on that stage and eat fire.

Some people in line near me were visibly upset. They spoke in whispers about all of the horrible possibilities and outcomes that just might happen to them or others, as a result of such a frivolous act.

Side by side, we ALL advanced toward the stage. We walked the same path. We climbed the same stairs. We stood in the same place. We were given the same instructions to follow and in the end achieved the same goal...WE ALL ATE FIRE!

Some of us walked in faith, enjoying every moment of every step taken. Some walked in fear, hating every step of the way. And, in the end, we all ate fire.

The only difference between us all was our individual journey to the same destination.

Take Flight
Even the peaceful magnificence of the white dove
must fly against the push of an unexpected gust of wind,
or venture forward through the adversity of inclement weather.
Yet this creature never hesitates to take flight.
It flies with faith and with assurance reaches its destination.

❧ ❧ ❧ ❧

The strength and endurance gained
as a result of a task that is difficult,
teaches us to realize that a challenge is only that...

❧ ❧ ❧ ❧

Fear presents to us the need for change,
and the first thing that must change is our choosing to feel that fear.

❧ ❧ ❧ ❧

We can accomplish anything we set our minds to,
if we believe we are capable and deserving of the accomplishment.

❧ ❧ ❧ ❧

Fear is the impenetrable wall we choose to build,
putting the ultimate barrier between ourselves and our goals.

❧ ❧ ❧ ❧

Faith, the extreme opposite of fear,
allows us to penetrate the confines,
grow through transition,
accept the gift of but another life lesson,
reach our well deserved destination
and rejoice for the opportunity to discover the miracle of change.

❧ ❧ ❧ ❧

Miracles are simply a change in perspective.
Realize the miracle...
and remember, it's all happening.

Contact Felice Cellini: felicecellini@hotmail.com

Teresa Velardi

Teresa is the Certified Chapter Leader for the Women's Prosperity Network in Northeast Pennsylvania.

She loves the relationships that are evolving in her life as well as the lives of her chapter members.

She shares, "Being authentic has brought me to a place in relationship to people of a caliber I would not have previously imagined." She is also a talented potter (a ceramic artist). You can see a sampling of her work at www.teresavelardi.com.

Teresa has overcome many obstacles, faced a multitude of challenges, and a number of life events that have *all* ultimately played a role in her personal growth and development. She loves God, her family and all the amazing people she calls friends. She is blessed with a sense of humor, and despite the adversities she has faced, has a joyful positive outlook. She has learned that we are who we are as a result of a lifetime of our personal choices, which together create our life experiences. She has also come to know that perspective makes a miraculous difference.

Teresa also loves to write and invites you to join her on her journey by visiting www.teresavelardi.blogspot.com. Share your experiences and comments there as well. Need a coach or an accountability partner? She says, "Let's talk. We are all in this together. When our lives touch, it's for a reason and God knows what He's doing so let's explore life's possibilities together."

Contact Teresa Velardi:
www.womensprosperitynetwork.com/nepa
teresavelardi@yahoo.com

Conquering Complacency – Consistency is the Key
by Teresa Velardi

Documenting my journey through life and transformation is something I love to do; it is an important part of who I am and the success I have had. Journaling is one place where I can BE REAL. I know it works and yet, there are times when I've stopped writing even though I know this behavior can result in the revitalization of old habits and ways of being that do not serve me, and do not contribute to my success.

What happens? Why is it when I am experiencing success and celebrating victories, I stop doing the very things that brought me to reach my goals?

The answer, I have discovered is so simple – consistency was replaced with complacency. I became "comfortable" and didn't think I had to do those things with as much fervor anymore. One day passes, then another, then another and before long, I am no longer on track to accomplish my goals. I have let go of successful habits, slipped into complacency, accepted the status quo and at times, been completely frustrated that I haven't met my goals. Baffling? Not really. Yet while I'm in the thick of it all, I have no clue. Am I the only one who has done this? Can you relate?

After several years of this type of yo-yo lifestyle, I have finally committed to replace complacency with consistency. I invite you to do the same. Experience the incredible results that await you!

While the commitment to consistency is applicable in all areas of my life, whether physical, financial, spiritual or emotional, and even relational, it has been so clearly evident in my journey to physical well-being. You see, about seven months ago I woke up and realized that I weighed 340 pounds, and on a not quite 5 foot 3 inch frame that is far from healthy. In fact, I think I would probably have to be about 8 feet tall to be proportionate and healthy at 340 pounds. I'll spare you the "story" behind all the things that happened in my life leading to this point. I know we all have a "story." Instead, I'll share with you the turning point that made me realize it was time for me to take total charge of my life.

I have been on the path of self-discovery and personal development for many years, and although I have made *huge* strides in many areas of my life, I still was not in tune with how I could apply what

I had learned to *every* facet of life. The truth is, I didn't want to look at the biggest part of myself, my physical body. I had lost and gained weight countless number of times and even with all the personal development seminars, self-help books, diet products I purchased, programs and clubs I joined, there I was, looking in the mirror at a reflection I didn't recognize, and moreover, did not represent the best me I could be.

It was time to enlist some one-on-one help.

I acquired a personal coach. For those of you who think you don't need one, this is a wakeup call. I thought the same thing, and look what I got myself into. At the very least, I suggest accountability partners. Connect with some people you can count on to hold you accountable for making the positive changes you desire in your life. Sometimes, we can't see the forest through the trees on our own. Accountability is key in changing your life!

I chose someone who was very straight forward, and asked several questions about many things that I didn't want to answer. Since I had invested a lot of money in the coaching, I figured I'd only be wasting my money and keeping myself from the life of my dreams if I didn't participate fully. Oh yes, I danced around the weight issue for as long as my coach would let me get away with it, because that's what I had always done. You know the definition of insanity, right? Doing the same thing over, and over again, and expecting a different result. I KNEW that. Also, I had heard SO many times, "if you do what you've always done, you'll get what you've always got." Knowledge without action is still only knowledge.

Then one day during a very emotional conversation, something changed. It was time for me to GET REAL with where I was, what I looked like, not only to myself, but to others as well, and how I truly felt about what I was learning about myself in direct relation to my body. I was encouraged to look at how this aspect of my life was creating unmanageability in other areas of my life. I had to identify the current and potential future consequences of not implementing positive action to facilitate change. It was no secret to my coach that *every* aspect of my life was being adversely affected. *I* was the one who *really* needed to become AWARE of the reality.

Now, don't think for one minute I didn't *know* that I was fat. I have a mirror that would probably have wanted to run out of the room screaming every time I stepped in front of it if it had legs that would carry it! The issue was ACCEPTANCE. I needed to *accept* that I was responsible for my image No matter what my "story" was, I was 100% responsible. I had to have that shift in my mindset before *anything* would change. And, the half-hearted way that I was doing things for six months before had only resulted in a very small change on the scale. Once I came to a place of acceptance and personal responsibility, it was time for some serious ACTION.

Then, came the challenge! My coach, whom I think is awesome, told me he wanted me to tell everyone how much I weighed.

"Post it on Twitter and Facebook," he said.

I replied, "What? You're kidding right?"

I knew he wasn't, and I was cringing with embarrassment at the response I just *knew* I was going to get.

And then, he said something that really hit me "Teresa, do you want to be better and live the life of your dreams? Or are you full of shit?" Those were his *exact* words.

"I have to pray about this for a while," I said.

I did, and when I couldn't find my own words to pray, I prayed the serenity prayer:

" God, Grant me the SERENITY to ACCEPT the things I cannot change,

The COURAGE to change the things I can, and the WISDOM to know the difference."

Finally, I had the courage. I didn't just want to blurt it out there on Facebook and Twitter though, so I created a blog to record my journey. What I realized in that time of thought, prayer, and meditation, was that I was not faceted, that all parts of me are connected. The physical, emotional, spiritual, financial and relational are all intertwined. There is harmony and ease when *all* are nurtured.

So, having surrendered some things, taken 100% responsibility for others, I was renewed with a greater faith, confidence, optimism and a new sense of direction in my life. I made a choice to create a focused food and exercise program that I consistently followed for months. I didn't do it alone though. I enlisted God's help, and I was held accountable by other people, resulting in a 70-pound reduction. Yes! I was on my way.

Then, complacency set in. I was little by little, stepping further away from the food plan that worked; thinking I had it under control, not taking the same amount of time and effort to prepare my meals properly. Furthermore, I did not maintain the consistent attention to detail that I gave the program in the beginning by implementing the practices that worked to bring success!

You know that familiar saying, "If it ain't broke, don't fix it." Here's what I realized: Sometimes thinking I can do things "my way" (the *old way*; that didn't work) comes creeping back ... slowly ... manipulating its way into the cracks and crevices of my life. It winds its way into the consistency, creating a complacent attitude. Then, gratefully, in a moment of clarity, AWARENESS strikes and the complacent attitude is interrupted.

I've learned the key to long term success, achieving goals and truly living the life of your dreams, is found in the focused, consistent, daily habits that lead to your goals and dreams.

What goals and dreams do you have? How often do you focus on them? Feel them as realistic, attainable and that you *are* worthy. You *do* deserve your goals and dreams. Practice focusing on your goals daily to keep you in the habit of working towards them. I am focusing daily on my goal of weighing 140 lbs., and my daily actions are consistent with bringing me to that goal. I nurture my faith in God. "I can do everything through Him who gives me strength." That passage from Philippians 4:13 is my favorite Bible verse. I wear it on my wrist as a bracelet to remind me of just that!

As I write this, I am renewing my commitment to consistency. Right now, as you read this, renew your commitment! Every day, renew your commitment to consistency! ACHIEVE REAL RESULTS. I've applied this principle to every area of my life. Taking the time each day to focus on what I want keeps me faithful to the consistent daily actions I must take in order to reach the goals I set for every aspect of my life. The difference *is* in the details.

FAILURE is *NOT* AN OPTION!

To Your Success and Prosperity!

Contact Teresa Velardi:

www.womensprosperitynetwork.com/nepa
teresavelardi@yahoo.com

Chapter 3

GOALS

"Dreams and goals are previews of coming attractions in your life. You are the scriptwriter, the star performer, and the producer of either an Oscar-winning epic, or a grade-B movie that someone else wrote and directed for you."~Dr. Dennis Waitley

Introduction
by Nancy Matthews

Visionaries dream big. "Visionaries with Guts" take action to turn their dreams into reality. Big dreams require big plans and systems to achieve them. Just as creating an Oscar-winning epic requires detailed plans, every scene carefully written and choreographed, your dreams and goals require the same detailed attention. Creating plans, reviewing, revising and implementing them are the keys to the long-term success you deserve. It's often been said, "People don't plan to fail, they fail to plan" and having a plan, and the persistence to stick to it will turn your dreams into reality. I love to turn my goals into games, with yearly, monthly and daily objectives, and celebrating each accomplishment along the way. Planning is fun and persistence pays off. Ensure your success by having a mentor, coach or an accountability partner to support you, and celebrate your victories with you.

Belinda Ellsworth

Belinda is a highly sought after, internationally renowned speaker and consultant, who combined 30 years of field experience with innovative strategies to create measurable results. With a direct sales career that started at an early age, Belinda began developing systems and strategies that allowed her to achieve major milestones as her career progressed. She excelled quickly and earned the distinction of becoming the youngest Sales Vice President in her company's history. In 1995 Belinda founded Step into Success as a way to live out her passion of empowering others to *step into their own success*. To date she has trained thousands of sales representatives and consulted with dozens of businesses ranging from startups to multi-million dollar companies, helping them develop revenue increasing programs.

Contact Belinda Ellsworth:
www.StepIntoSuccess.com

Visionary Goal Setting
by Belinda Ellsworth

When I was first approached about this project and the subject of visionaries, I was very excited because I believe that being a visionary ranks as one of the most important criteria for achieving success. I also believe that one of the most important qualities of an effective leader is to build vision in others. So, what does it mean to be a visionary, and what skill sets does that require? How does one really build vision in others? Are we all able to do that?

We all know how important it is to set goals. Yet, we really have to look at the difference between goal setting and having a vision. Goals are generally short-term benchmarks that you would like to achieve in order to complete a particular task. So often, people confuse goal setting with achieving success. It certainly will contribute to your success, but once achieved, if you don't continue to set new goals, you will remain exactly where you are.

Vision, on the other hand, is seeing the big picture—having a clear idea of where you want to be one year from now or three years, five years, or possibly ten years from now. When you have a real idea or picture of what you want your life or business to look like three to ten years from now, goal setting becomes much easier and a lot more fun. There is energy created in the task because you have purpose. I have always set goals for the year and then broke those down quarterly, monthly, weekly, daily, and even hourly. But, I have also always had a three-year, five-year, and ten-year plan or vision. My benchmarks have always been in 10-year increments.

When I was twenty-years-old, I set a clear picture of where I wanted to be by the time I turned thirty. Things changed, my goals changed, my career changed, company product lines changed, and I adjusted my goals accordingly, but not my vision. By the time I was thirty, I was exactly where I envisioned myself to be. Every decade I've followed the same pattern, and it keeps the journey exciting and me on track towards success.

Now let's look at some strong statistics about this subject. It used to be that about 20% of people set goals in their life. That's where we get the 20/80 rule – 20% of the people do 80% of the work. It's that 20% that have an idea of what they are working toward. The newest statistics show that only about 13% of people will naturally set goals. This is why, as a leader, it is so important that we help individuals set goals and clarify their vision. Productivity almost always goes hand-in-hand with goal setting and working toward that vision. Random acts get you random results. Those who act with intention and purpose get their desired results.

Previous statistics showed that only 10% of people had a clear vision of what they wanted to achieve. Sadly, new statistics show only about 3% of people have any vision at all of what they want their life to look like in the future. This lack of planning impacts all areas of a person's life—financial, personal, and business. Another startling statistic is only 1%-2% of people have the natural ability to build vision in others. If this is one of the greatest qualities of a leader, what does this mean for the 98% of other people—especially those that want to be a great leader? To gain this skill of building vision in others, those prospective leaders will have to seek it out, find mentors, learn it, and apply this concept in their lives. Some people are born with it, and others can develop this quality over time. However, you must be able to build vision in your own life first, before you can inspire and build vision in others.

I feel very fortunate and blessed that I was born with the gift of inspiring others, building them up, and getting people to believe in the greater good or to see the benefit of working hard toward something that is currently out of reach. I have been doing this since I was a child. That is how I know it is a gift and a natural ability. As I matured, I realized that this is what sets apart the great leaders from the good ones. In my efforts to become a better leader, I have made it my mission to learn as much as I can about the subject, to seek out mentors, discover their methods and emulate them. To be really great at anything, we always have to continue to learn in order to grow.

When I first considered a speaking career, I had been encouraged by other speakers who had heard me present my training at the convention where they were the keynote speaker. Over the course of a year, they encouraged me to go out on my own. I started to think about what my program would look like and who would be in the audience. I started to have a vision of where I could be in five years, or by the time I was forty. I was making a very good salary with substantial bonuses; however, I was not happy. I did not feel in my heart that I was reaching my full potential, and I could not envision myself there for the next twenty years of my life, so I decided to make a change. I was hopeful and had a great belief in myself and it certainly helped having the endorsement of two well-known speakers.

Within just a few weeks of leaving my job, I received a phone call for an interview with another company for a position similar to what I had just left. The pay and bonuses were much higher, but I just wasn't ready to take it and abandon my dream or vision. Taking the job would have been instant gratification in the moment, good pay, easier lifestyle, but it did not contribute to my dream or vision of where I wanted to be by forty, so I declined the offer.

The individual was irritated because they really wanted me to work for their company and said, "Why would you do this. You have nothing, and I'm offering you a lot."

I replied, "I have a strong belief in myself and vision of where I want to be, and I know that, if I work hard, I will get there." I let them know I appreciated the offer and left. I also received pressure from my family to take the easy road, but my commitment to my dream only strengthened. Being a visionary takes guts. It isn't the easy way out, it isn't the sure thing, and it clearly isn't instant gratification. It is knowing what you want and believing without a shadow of a doubt that you'll do what it takes to make it happen.

When I began my speaking career, I had been in sales and very successful at it for sixteen years. I had a clear vision of where I wanted my new career to be in three, five, and ten years. My goal for that first year was to have six paid speaking engagements per month. As I made those initial calls and received no after no after no, as well as many "Who are you? What do you do?" responses, I became discouraged. I kept my vision but I changed my goals. Getting six paid speaking engagement in a month from zero was pretty lofty. It wasn't as easy as I thought.

There were moments in that time frame I thought about taking that job, but I started to envision a brick wall, and every call I made, whether it was just a connection or a referral to someone else or even a "no thank you." I imagined one brick coming down. I literally drew a picture of it. I began to get excited about knocking the wall down, not about a scheduled speaking engagement. In the first several months, I only had two bookings, but by the fourth month, the number began to climb. Within six months, I had four bookings a month and it continued to grow from there. It grew because I kept knocking bricks out of that wall. That vision helped me through a challenging time to stay hopeful, and believe in myself when others would have given up.

That was fifteen years ago, and I have had a very successful career as a speaker and trainer. The exciting thing is there is still so much ahead. I just turned forty-nine, and as I sat and looked at my vision of where I wanted to be at fifty, my life is pretty much just as I had pictured it. Where I live, my dream home, my income, my family and where they are in their lives, and my business. There were lots of changes in those ten years, as well as ups and downs, but amazingly the end result is very much how I envisioned it. I am excited about my next ten year vision and where that will lead me.

I have found it to be true at twenty, thirty, forty and fifty—success is a journey and along that journey we are sure to have speed bumps, detours, and roadblocks. Life is full of challenges, crisis, and change, but it's the people who have a destination in mind, a clear picture of where they are going, who keep moving. The people who contributed to this book are these people; visionaries—visionaries with guts; I am honored to be among them.

Contact Belinda Ellsworth:
www.StepIntoSuccess.com

Dan Roose

Dan Roose is a Business Development Consultant and the Founder of No Greater Wealth, LLC. He specializes in helping businesses and individuals set realistic goals and build effective plans to achieve those goals. He is a retired Army Lieutenant Colonel, taught for 3 years as an assistant professor at the College of Williams and Mary and holds a B.S. in Economics and a Master's degree in Human Resource Management. He is married and has eleven children, ages six- months old to seventeen-years-old.

Contact Dan Roose:
www.nogreaterwealth.com
Dan@nogreaterwealth.com

Setting and Achieving Realistic Goals
by Dan Roose

When you ask most people what their goals are more often than not, you will get a blank stare or a thoughtful gaze. Sometimes the person will gladly tell you about their goals. The problem is they are vague at best and when you wade a little farther into the subject, the person you are talking with cannot tell you for the life of them how they intend to reach them. Why is it so hard to set realistic goals and actually reach them? Goal setting is easy and everyone can do it. Your goals are just the destinations. All you need is a map to get you there. The tools in this chapter will help you build your map.

A *goal* is an aim; an end; *the result or achievement toward which effort is directed.* You must know from the beginning that your goal will take effort. *Effort* is *the amount of exertion expended for a specific purpose.* The amount of effort will vary depending on the person and the goals they set. The most important elements in achieving your goal are effort, perseverance, and more effort.

There are five steps needed to set and reach realistic goals:

1. Establish a Goal

2. Backwards Plan

3. Get Accountability

4. Build a Team

5. Gather Information

Step one, You Need a GOAL. Not shocking, you must have an end in mind. Goals can be set for almost every area of your life. You can have financial, marriage, parenting, and exercise goals, just to name a few. For the purposes of this article, I am going to use financial goals for my examples.

Goals MUST BE WRITTEN DOWN! If it is not written down, it does not exist. Take some time to sit down and write out your goals. Don't sit around looking at a piece of paper or your computer for an hour. Start writing! Dream! Dream big dreams! Most people set their goals way too low. You want your goals to be achievable and that is different for everyone. Now evaluate your dreams and write down your goals with dates for completion. Remember GOALS CAN ALWAYS BE CHANGED! They are your goals and you can modify them any way you wish.

Below is an example of a set of financial goals I have set for myself, and my family:

- Have a $10 million net worth by 2019
- Have an endowment fund with $2 million for ministry work by 2019
- Be completely debt free by 2015 (includes house)
- Buy a piece of property with 25+ acres by 2019
- Build a house that is paid for
- Have an Arena size football field on the property
- Build a convention hall for ministry work (ballroom and worship dance) meetings, weddings, conferences

Your reaction to my first goal may have been, "I can't do that." If that was you, then you need to dream bigger. I love to dream and I am willing to do the work it takes to reach my dreams. Notice that I made my goals measurable by being specific, giving them dollar values and dates. Your goals need to be measurable and specific, so you can build a plan to achieve them.

After you have written your goals down you should put them aside for a day to think about them. Show them to your spouse or to friends you trust and see what they think. Give some thought to revising them. Once you are done with this step, it's time to TAKE ACTION! You can make a flawless plan, but without the necessary action, hard work and perseverance it will only be a pretty plan. You must decide from the beginning that you will put in the effort needed.

Step two is my favorite part. Build a Backwards Plan. You already use backwards planning you just don't use that name to describe it. For example, if you are going to go to a sporting event or a concert on a work day, you would have to make sure you had the day off, filled the car up with gas the day before, bought the tickets to the game prior to leaving, talked with your friends, or whomever was coming with you to coordinate for car pooling and food, and so on. Backwards planning for your goals is more deliberate and you may need some help to make sure you cover everything.

Building a backwards plan is just working backwards from the goal to where you are today and placing intermediate goals along the way to help guide you on your path to success. They are like intersections on your map. As you build your backwards plan, you will be able to visualize how you can reach your goals and this will give you confidence. Remember your plan is a work in progress and can be modified. As you move toward achieving your goal, information and situations will change. When this happens, update and fine-tune your plan. This is just a detour in the road. DO NOT STOP taking action, be creative and modify your goals if you have to, but keep working!

I am using more than one way to reach the financial goals I identified above. I am using several different methods to increase my passive income and increase my cash flow. Below I will highlight one of the avenues helping me to achieve those financial goals. Here is part of my backwards plan for my XOWii (pronounced ZOW-WEE) network marketing business. I joined this company in October of 2009, the first month it opened. My vision for starting this business was to allow me to retire from the US Army by increasing my passive income in a very short time, and replace my active duty military pay.

My 2-year goals for XOWii:
>Be at the highest rank by July 2011.
>Earn at least $50,000 per month by July 2011.
>Be completely out of debt (minus my house) by July 2011.

My 1-year goals XOWii:
>Increase in rank every 8 weeks.
>Replace my active duty military pay by October 2010.
>Achieve the free BMW award by December 2010.

My January 2010 (monthly) goals for XOWii:
>Achieve the rank of XOWii 600 by the end of January 2010.
>Talk to five people a week about the opportunity.
>Enroll two people a month.
>Send my goals to my up line so they can hold me accountable.
>Continue to read one book a month about Network Marketing.
>Help my team members achieve their goals.

My monthly goals change based on how well I did during the last month. Sometimes I fall short of my monthly goals and sometimes I exceed them. That last statement is very important when working on your goals. Just because you have met your goals for the month or reached one of your intermediate goals early does not mean you should kick back and coast. This is the time for you to seize the momentum and keep your high level of success going. You will have times when you fall behind so ensure you maximize the times you are ahead.

Step three is Accountability. This is essential and takes a lot of discipline. It is an area where a lot of people fall short. In most jobs, there is a proverb that says, "The workers only do what the supervisor is willing to check." Your goals are the same way. It is hard to answer to yourself, and excuses destroy success. You can always justify why you did something, or why you have not completed a task. That is why you need someone outside of your immediate family to hold you accountable. If you are married, your spouse should be one of your accountability partners. It has been my experience that someone less emotionally tied to you, can also provide excellent insights into how you are doing. Once you have made a commitment to set and achieve your goals, you need to find at least one person, two is better, whom you trust and have them hold you accountable to your goals.

Your accountability partner needs to have a copy of your written goals, your backwards plan, and a list of questions that you provide them. I recommend at least five, but not more than ten questions. These questions can and should change as you move towards your goal. The list of questions should include all the areas where you know you are weak. Put them on an index card and have your accountability partner ask them to you at least once every two weeks, but preferably every week. This should be done face to face if possible, last about thirty minutes, and you should take notes. Having helped hundreds of people set and achieve their goals; I can tell you that the more consistent your accountability, the more effective your effort. Let your accountability partner add questions to your list if they want. Give them permission to ask you the tough questions and tell you when they think you are failing to meet your goals. Without accountability, it is almost impossible to reach your goals.

I have a good friend and business partner who I use to hold me accountable to my XOWii business goals. I provide him with my overall goals and my monthly goals. Some of the questions I have him ask me include:

- How many people did you talk to about the XOWii opportunity this week?
- How many people have you hosted a meeting for this week?
- How many people have you given samples to this week?
- How much reading have you done this week?

It is great if you can use one accountability partner for multiple areas in your life, but having more than one is helpful as well. For example, I have a different accountability partner for my marriage and parenting goals.

Step four is Building a Team. There are no "Lone Rangers" where achieving success is concerned. Part of your team can include a tax specialist, real estate lawyer, virtual assistant, web designer, or marriage counselor, to name a few. Your goals will help you determine who needs to be on your team. A mentor is a critical team member. Find people who have already done what you are trying to do and ask them if they will mentor you. Make sure you only use people who are positive and motivating. Achieving your goals is hard enough; you do not need a bunch of naysayers on your team bringing you down. People on your team can be your friends and family members, as well as paid professionals.

There is something you should know as you start dreaming and setting your goals. You will have family members and friends who tell you that you are crazy and that you will never make it. Those people, even though they love you, are roadblocks on your way to your destination. You are going to have to make some tough choices on this one as you move forward. Now your immediate family, for example, your spouse should never be a roadblock because you should be working with them and setting your goals together. Since they are on this journey of life with you, the two of you should be on the same road. Having you and your spouse driving down two separate roads will be an extremely difficult roadblock to overcome. As for the rest, you may have to consider limiting the time you spend with them, or even finding new friends who will support you.

As you build your team and mentor relationships, make sure you are very specific when you explain what you want from them. This will make it easy for them to know how they can help you. Once you find someone you want to add to your team, set up a thirty-minute appointment with them. Then, before the appointment make a list of interview questions. This will help you stay on topic and show them that you value their time. Finally, be ready to reciprocate and support your team when they need your help. Achieving goals is a team sport.

Step five is Gathering Information. You must be a student of your own success. Commit thirty minutes to an hour every evening or every other evening to your education. Get a notebook and write down things you are learning and where you found the information. Read books and magazine articles, do research on the Internet, attend webinars and go to live seminars; this is a continuous process. The more you know about what you are trying to achieve the better decisions you will make. There is no substitute for knowledge. It gives you more tools to use, helps you see upcoming problems and prepares you with strategies when challenges arise. This reduces the roadblocks and ultimately reduces the time it takes to achieve your goals.

These five steps to set and achieve your goals may seem challenging when you first start, but if you will just start by writing something down on paper, it will get easier as you move forward. Use the tools of planning, accountability, teamwork, along with plenty of perseverance and you will meet your goals. The only people who truly fail are the ones who quit. As Winston Churchill said, "Never, never, never give up!

Contact Dan Roose:
www.nogreaterwealth.com
Dan@nogreaterwealth.com

Danielle Cortes DeVito

Danielle Cortes DeVito is a professional speaker, who inspires companies and individuals to live a healthy and productive life. She has captivated audiences across the U.S. speaking about her passion of living a heart healthy lifestyle and preventing heart disease and strokes. Danielle has 15 years experience in the emergency medical field and 7 years as a spokesperson for the American Heart Association. She has taken her expertise and put together a powerful keynote speech and a workplace wellness consulting company.

Danielle is a passionate and dynamic speaker whose unique blend of innovative ideas, and experience with real-life emergencies will ensure that your next conference, workshop or training event is an uplifting and informative yet, entertaining experience.

A partial client list includes IKEA, Shell Oil, American Heart Association, Argonne National Laboratory, and Association of Black Cardiologists.

Contact Danielle Cortes DeVito:
www.DanielleSpeaks.com
www..Artofhealthyleadership.com

The Art of Healthy Leadership™
by Danielle Cortes DeVito

Let's face it. We have all had adversity in our lives which has knocked us off our path. Maybe it is the loss of a job, or loved one. These are challenges that are placed upon us. The great thing about life is that it is a journey. You have the choice either to allow circumstances to run your life or to move through the experience to your goals, dreams, and destiny.

In the spring of 1992, an accident changed my life. It occurred while I was taking public transportation to school. I was a senior in high school, and in the process of embarking on my own journey into the collegiate world. Right in front of the bus stop a four-car collision occurred. It left me frightened. The ambulances showed up a few minutes later to tend to the wounded.

What happened next changed my life. Two women got out of the ambulance. They handled it with grace, and within ten minutes, the scene was clear. I was able to continue on my way. I knew at that very moment I wanted to help people when they were in danger.

Later on that night, I told the traumatic story to my mother and grandmother and announced that I wanted to be a paramedic. They responded with disdain. Their reason was that it was too dangerous. I never saw those ambulance women again, although I see them mentally every time someone asks me why I chose my occupation. From then on, I transformed my fears into inspiration. I became a loving mother, paramedic, and health activist.

I learned along the way that in order to obtain good physical health, you must be fit in your mind, mentally fit to carry out your goals and dreams, those which we aspire to carry out in our lifetime. The purpose of the *Art of Healthy Leadership*™ is to lead a purposeful and healthy life. I'll explain the three components of this concept to you.

The first component to *Art of Healthy Leadership*™ is Purpose. In order to accomplish your goals, physically or otherwise, you must know and define your purpose. Have you ever asked yourself, "Why am I working in this job?, Why am I now 20 pounds overweight?, How did I get here?" Years go by and we have passed up so much.

I believe everyone deserves to live a healthy and purposeful life. If you don't know your purpose, you will find yourself on the outside looking in. You must constantly question where you are and where you are going. In order to lead a healthy life you must have a dynamic relationship with yourself, taking the time you need to recharge and to take care of your body.

I meet so many people who take care of everyone else or excel in their careers. They say, "I don't have time to work out, eat healthy or even sleep." That's not true. They have chosen not to work out, eat healthy or sleep. Of course, things come up. Kids get sick, there is an emergency deadline at work or a snow blizzard and you can't get to the gym or grocery store.

We have to stop using distractions as an excuse. If you don't take care of yourself, you won't be around to care for your loved ones, and share wonderful moments with them. The job will still be there long after we are all gone. Trust me. We are given only one body. There is no restart button. You wouldn't put cheap gas in a Mercedes Benz. Your body is always keeping score.

Your purpose must be your own. Your passion is formulated from deep within yourself. What's your purpose? Who do you admire? And why? What do you enjoy doing? What's the vision for your company? Your family? If you always wanted to write, take a writer's course. Be creative and stay on your path to greatness. When you have your purpose and are following your passion, that's when you can lead in all areas of your life. When you feel good about yourself, you can lead yourself, your team and your family through crisis and beyond.

The second component to *Art of Healthy Leadership*™ is Prepare. The dictionary says: "Preparedness refers to the state of being prepared for specific or unpredictable events or situations." Preparedness is an important quality in achieving goals and in avoiding and mitigating negative outcomes. Take charge of your life and health by taking precise and bold actions. Planting the seeds of success every day is critical. Take a lunch and snacks with you so you don't resort to junk food. Keep a gym bag in the car with 2-3 workout outfits. Take the stairs instead of the elevator. Start a walking club at work. When others see you doing this, they will follow, because you are a healthy leader.

You and your team must be prepared to handle obstacles. Your team may consist of your coworkers, family or support group. You must examine your failures objectively and move to your success. Mistakes and failures are just opportunities to learn what's not working and how to do better.

The Department of Labor says that "every year, 200,000 Americans die of sudden cardiac arrest in the workplace." Can you imagine how many lives could be saved if everyone knew CPR and every office had an Automatic External Defibrillator? Being prepared moves you from an ordinary to an extraordinary mindset.

The third component to the *Art of Healthy Leadership*™ is Productivity. One of my favorite movies is *Rudy*. Rudy is a young man who dreamed of playing football for Notre Dame University. Every step of the way people told him it was impossible because he wasn't smart enough and he was too small. At 160 pounds, Rudy stood 5 feet, 6 inches tall and was labeled with a learning disability. Year after year, his application to Notre Dame met with disappointment.

He studied day and night. He trained constantly to become stronger and faster. Everyone told him he was insane and it would not happen. In 1975 Rudy played football for Notre Dame University in front of his family and peers and was carried off the field by teammates. Rudy had done everything in his power to make his dream come true.

Producing the results you say you want is not always easy. It takes more than hard work and determination. It's healthy habitual behaviors. You can't keep doing the same things you have been doing and expect to get different results. Your goals appear when you have committed to never giving up.

Are you doing everything in your power to create the results you want? Start today by finding your purpose, preparing and producing the results you want with your health and life. Master the *Art of Healthy Leadership*™ by being courageous and holding the mental image that there are no limits to what you can accomplish.

Contact Danielle Cortes DeVito:

www.DanielleSpeaks.com
www..Artofhealthyleadership.com

Chapter 4

BALANCE: GOING FOR WHAT YOU WANT IN ALL AREAS OF YOUR LIFE

"Just as your car runs more smoothly and requires less energy to go faster and farther when the wheels are in perfect alignment, you perform better when your thoughts, feelings, emotions, goals and values are in balance." ~Brian Tracy

Introduction
by Nancy Matthews

During the time that I was climbing the ladder of success, running a full service title agency, mortgage brokerage and real estate investment company, as a single parent and determined to "make it," my dear friend, Sam, gave me a gift that changed my life. It was a T-Shirt. A simple white T-Shirt with the saying, "The most important things in life *aren't* things." Wow! Talk about a wake-up call. I discovered that my life and my priorities were completely out of balance. I was out of shape, 40 pounds overweight and never exercised. Quality time with my children was dinner at the local restaurant where we ate almost every night and I rarely made time to simply relax and "be." I was on the fast track alright, but the question was, the fast track to where?

I am a passionate person and whatever I choose to do, I do with full enthusiasm, energy and gusto (as I'm sure you do too.) Creating and keeping balance in my life requires dedication and attention to the "things" that matter most. And yes, the things that matter most aren't things. As I create my daily life now, my priority is to dedicate time to reading, journaling, exercise and spending time with my family. Now when my daughter, Megan, sends a text message that says, "Want to go to Dunkin Donuts?" I happily respond, "Absolutely!" grateful to spend time with her. And, on most days, I skip the donut.

Belinda Ellsworth

Belinda is a highly sought after, internationally renowned speaker and consultant, who combined 30 years of field experience with innovative strategies to create measurable results. With a direct sales career that started at an early age, Belinda began developing systems and strategies that allowed her to achieve major milestones as her career progressed. She excelled quickly and earned the distinction of becoming the youngest Sales Vice President in her company's history. In 1995 Belinda founded Step into Success as a way to live out her passion of empowering others to *step into their own success*. To date she has trained thousands of sales representatives and consulted with dozens of businesses ranging from startups to multi-million dollar companies, helping them develop revenue increasing programs.

Contact Belinda Ellsworth:
www.StepIntoSuccess.com

A Simple Time Management Solution for Accomplishing More
by Belinda Ellsworth

A comment I often hear from business owners across the country is, "There is just not enough time in the day to get everything done." Managing our time takes on new meaning in this fast-paced business world, a world where we're accessible 24/7, often working with those in different time zones, and receiving hundreds of e-mails a day. It's easy to get caught up in answering e-mails or phone calls and handling daily distractions, and we sometimes end up feeling just as overwhelmed as we did at the beginning of the day. We cannot add more hours to the day. However, we can implement time management solutions that will allow us to work efficiently and stay accountable, while helping us accomplish what we set out to do at the beginning of each day. Achieving our daily goals will help create the momentum to attain our weekly and monthly goals, moving us closer to our vision of success.

For those of us who work remotely or alone, the lack of structure and schedule, and a perception of having an abundant amount of time on our hands can keep us from focusing on necessary tasks. Working out of your home presents the daily challenges of staying focused on your business and refraining from managing your household. An office environment can present another set of time-stealing factors. Have you ever experienced one of those days packed with interruptions or back-to-back meetings, and next thing you know, the day has gone by and you feel like you did not accomplish a thing? Even more challenging can be managing time when working from different locations: you "work-from-home" some days and "go into the office" on others. Each situation presents us with different obstacles that could prevent us from maximizing the best use of our time.

Before you can decide where you need to improve you must look at your day. What percent of your time is spent on day-to-day details? Prospecting new clients? Customer follow-up? The revenue-generating activities we're not devoting our time to – often in the form of phone calls we *really* need to be making – are what we truly need in order to move our businesses or projects forward. Many of us network and meet new contacts at various meetings. However, do you take the time to follow up with a phone call? Do you follow up with an interested prospect? Did you close the sale?

Moving business forward — even creating new business — involves establishing and fostering relationships. Often, that means getting on the phone, whether to find new clients, cultivate networks, conduct business transactions, or provide superior customer care. Many times these important calls fall by the wayside in a busy schedule. But it's these essential tasks that ultimately result in revenue and create profitable and sustainable businesses. Implementing an easy system that allows us to focus our energies on revenue-generating activities will help us work efficiently, keep ourselves accountable and allow us to achieve our desired results faster.

Through the years as my business began to grow, I found myself creating a monthly, weekly, daily, even hourly schedule to keep me focused on what I needed to get accomplished each day. This kept me on track and helped me reach my short and long-term goals. This consistent effort resulted in growing my business every month. As many watched my business grow, they asked me what I was doing to achieve such incredible results. It was then that I decided to create The Power Hour to teach others this adaptable system and to help them achieve the success they were looking for.

In a nutshell, a *power hour* is a period of focused activity evenly divided between the four primary drivers of your businesses — the four most important revenue-generating activities.

Identify the Four Drivers

Look at your business and determine your four most important revenue-generating activities. This system has been very popular in direct sales business models because it helps independent sales consultants focus on the phone calls necessary to keep their businesses running smoothly. In one such industry, the four types of calls are: to book parties, calls to coach the hostesses, calls to provide customer service for their existing clients, and calls to follow-up on leads.

People in other professional roles have different needs. For example, a realtor might determine the four categories, or *drivers,* of the revenue in the business are: prospecting calls to potential clients, calls to former customers to ask for referrals, calls to current customers to check on their progress, and other relationship-building calls, such as to a mortgage broker or title company who could generate new business.

Regardless of the specifics of an industry or work role, there are always primary revenue-generating activities. The first step is getting a handle on what they are for you.

Organize the Information

Every minute of a power hour needs to be devoted specifically to the revenue-generating activity, so it is essential to have a system in place to track all of your daily activity, and to schedule client follow-up and other related tasks. It doesn't matter if it is as simple as four color-coded folders or as complex as a contact management system. Find a structure that you are willing to follow that helps you become more efficient with your time. The type of system you choose is irrelevant; the most important thing is that you commit to using it, no matter what. How can you prioritize tasks and schedule your day without an organized system to track your steps and determine/remind you of what your next steps need to be? Many times having a system in place that keeps you organized can be the difference between businesses that fail and those that prosper.

Apply the Discipline

I have been training clients in this system for years and have found what often trips people up is that they do not devote their time to the different categories evenly. We all have activities that we enjoy – calling up old clients to catch up – and activities that we tend to put off – like making cold calls. The hidden power of this system is reflected in the results you will see by dividing your time equally between the four categories, working only on those specific tasks during that time period, thereby increasing your productivity. This prevents one particular task from taking up all of your time, creating a balanced approach to building your business.

Whether it's an actual hour divided into 15-minute sections, or a longer period, the discipline of focusing on a specific objective for a pre-determined period of time and stopping as soon as it's over will help you accomplish more. It's much like anything we "make" ourselves do. Just think, "I can do anything for 15 minutes," dive in and make the calls you loathe, knowing that you get to stop and move on soon. The power hour will provide the discipline and structure you need to keep moving, get the important things done and accomplish your goals.

Make the Time and Make It Yours

Use the system, but implement it in chunks of time that suit your needs. Some people find that on heavy meeting days, planning a power hour in advance is helpful, because they know the rest of the day won't be productive – or at least not productive in the areas that drive the revenue of their business. Impromptu power hours work well for people who find themselves checking the clock, realizing it's after 2:30 PM, no lunch yet, and nothing accomplished for the day. Others find that to keep their business booming they routinely begin and end their workdays with solid power hours. The flexibility allows you to create a schedule that is right for you.

Regardless of how you use it, the system creates structured time that is about nothing other than your main revenue-generating activities. No answering the phone, chatting with co-workers, taking walks to the snack machine, or going downstairs for another cup of coffee. It's about accountability and honoring the time you've committed, knowing that when the time is up, you can walk away from the phone or the desk and do whatever you feel you need to do. Good news *and* bad news for incurable multi-taskers: Your most common distractions will almost always be waiting for you when you're done.

What It Will Mean to Your Business

As I've mentioned before, this is the system I used to successfully build my business. Time after time, I've seen solid growth, innovation, and improved efficiency in the businesses of other people who have adopted a power hour approach. Notice that as you identify the four categories in your business, one of them tends to be a task that you do not particularly enjoy. It's rare that the tasks completed during the power hours are anyone's *favorite* activities, but they are quite important, if not essential, for generating revenue. After you create these new habit patterns and see success, you will eventually become comfortable and you will enjoy doing them more because your confidence level will grow. Over time, we find that the work done in one category creates more opportunity in the others. The prospecting calls convert to clients, which result in customer care calls. The power hour ends up fueling all aspects of the business and this daily routine provides the structure needed to manage your time in an efficient and balanced way that actually "makes you money."

So, if you find yourself at the end of a busy day commenting,

"There is just not enough time in the day to get everything done," look at your time management skills and ask yourself a few questions. Are you managing your time, making the most out of every day? Or do you begin each day with a list of goals you never complete? If you have set goals for yourself and continually fail to achieve them, then consider changing the way you manage your day. Don't continue doing what you have been doing if it is not moving you toward your vision of success. Keep yourself accountable every day by implementing the Power Hour system into your daily routine. We cannot create a longer day, but we can learn ways to work smarter and more efficiently. This will result in growing our business and giving us back time into our day.

Contact Belinda Ellsworth:
www.StepIntoSuccess.com

Dan Roose

Dan Roose is a Business Development Consultant and the Founder of No Greater Wealth, LLC. He specializes in helping businesses and individuals set realistic goals and build effective plans to achieve those goals. He is a retired Army Lieutenant Colonel, taught for 3 years as an assistant professor at the College of Williams and Mary and holds a B.S. in Economics and a Master's degree in Human Resource Management. He is married and has eleven children, ages six-months-old to seventeen-years-old.

Contact Dan Roose:
www.nogreaterwealth.com
Dan@nogreaterwealth.com

How to Have Successful Relationships
by Dan Roose

Vibrant relationships don't just happen; they are created with work and perseverance. Time and intention are the keys to building relationships, while self-sacrifice and looking out for the needs of others maintains vibrant relationships. Being intentional has been the most important tool I have used in building successful relationships. My 20-year marriage to Penny has been an adventure. We have strolled along through easy times and have trudged through trials, but never have I stopped striving to maintain a rich and fun partnership. There is never a dull moment with eleven children six-months-old to seventeen-years-old, and keeping their hearts has been a challenge and a joy. As a retired US Army Lieutenant Colonel with twenty-four years of service, I understand how hard it can be to maintain relationships, especially when deployed for a year at a time or my schedule is demanding, not to mention all the children's activities. You must be intentional when it comes to building relationships.

Most people do not know what it looks like to be intentional with relationships. I know I didn't understand it when I was starting out. This article will lay out a practical guide to building the relationships that will encourage you and help everyone around you achieve greater success.

First, have a family meeting. Bring a pen, notebook and a calendar. Ask your family what activities they would enjoy doing with you. Write down their ideas in the notebook. This will get you headed down the right path. To have quality relationships, you have to be willing to sacrifice your desires and be willing to do the things the other person wants to do.

Second, fill out a calendar. Record all the activities that your spouse and kids attend. This includes sports practices, music lessons, and special events, to name a few. Once you complete your calendar and you fully understand the time requirements of your family, you are ready for step three.

Third, make a plan. This will take a little time and you will be making some tough choices. As you look at what time remains to build relationships, you may have to eliminate some of the things you do and ask your family to give up some things they do so that the relationships become a higher priority. You have heard it said that every kid spells love, T-I-M-E. Nothing has changed since and we are all kids at heart.

Your plan has to be flexible and needs to be a top priority for it to work. You must choose on a daily basis to grow your relationships. If the only time you have on the calendar to spend time with your oldest daughter is Saturday morning, then that is when you spend time with her. These relationships will last your entire lifetime whether they are good or bad, so you might as well make them rich and enduring.

Write your relationship building times on your personal calendar. Call them appointments. This will give you permission to say, "I have an appointment," and give it more priority than you have in the past. When conflicts arise never cancel these appointments, re-schedule them. This is non-negotiable.

Fourth, have a second family meeting to coordinate and schedule these relationship-building appointments. Have everyone who has a personal calendar bring it with them. At this meeting, you need to lay out your intent to your family and work out any conflicts that you may not have considered. Then, ensure that everyone adds these new appointments to his or her calendar. This will help immensely to ensure the plan's success.

Fifth, <u>WORK THE PLAN</u>! As Nike Corporation says, "Just do it." When you are spending time with your wife, family and friends, you must turn off your cell phone, get away from your computer and give your undivided attention to the person you are spending time with. The chart below is an example of a 90-day plan that I use to maintain and grow vibrant, life giving relationships in my family.

90 DAY FAMILY GOALS

Goal	Steps to fulfillment	SEP		OCT					NOV					DEC	
		21	28	4	1	1	18	25	1	8	15	22	29	5	12
Relationship w/Penny															
date night (Tuesday)	1 x week	X	X	X	X	X	X	X	X	X	X	X	X	X	X
couch time	3 x week	X	X	X	X	X	X	X	X	X	X	X	X	X	X
kiss and greet	5 x week	X	X	X	X	X	X	X	X	X	X	X	X	X	X
Relationship w/Samantha 16															
outing with Samantha	rotating		X												
encouragement	1 note every 2 wks	X		X			X		X		X		X		X
read a book aloud together	1x every 2 wks		X			X		X		X		X		X	
Relationship w/Mark 5															
outing with Mark	rotating									X					
bike ride	1x every 2 weeks	X		X			X		X		X		X		X
board game	1x every 2 weeks		X			X		X		X		X		X	

This is just a snap shot of a plan for my wife, my sixteen-year-old daughter, and my five-year-old old son. My chart does encompass all eleven children and I review it every 90 days. This chart allows me to stay focused and ensures that I am spending my time effectively. As I complete each appointment, I circle it on the chart to show it is complete.

The **Sixth and final step,** adjust your plan so it works. To persevere through the challenging times, you will have to make tough choices. There is no magical formula; be creative. It is your responsibility to be intentional, and to take action to create the life-giving, abundant relationships we all crave.

I have learned over the years how to make this process work better. Striving to make and keep my spouse my best friend has been the number one thing I have done for my marriage and family. Below are the activities I have used:

• First, I pray with my wife every day. There really is no substitute for having a firm foundation in your spiritual life.

• Second, I have worked with her to establish a shared vision, common goals and a mission statement for our family. We have spent time reading marriage and parenting books together, attending marriage enrichment conferences, and, we do lots of family activities. Taking my wife out on a "date" is her favorite activity. I take her out once a week, because I continually want to rekindle the thoughts and emotions that were there when we first got married.

• Third, I look to do things for her that let her know that I think she is special. An example includes, making her coffee from time to time. This may not seem like much, but I don't drink coffee so she knows I was thinking of her when I take the TIME to make her coffee. It is an example of being 'other people focused.'

My wife and I believe all children desperately need and want a strong relationship with their parents, but they do not always know how to do it. As the parent, you need to be a student of your children so you can make suggestions about how you will spend time with them. For your younger children ages 3 to 8, it could be almost anything. For example, reading them a book, playing the tickle game, playing catch, playing cars on the floor, playing dolls or diner, doing a puzzle, board games, going on a bike ride, pushing them on a swing, or wrestling, just to name a few.

For older children ages 8 to 17, they will have many of their own ideas. Some of the activities I do with my older children include: reading and talking about topics of interest with them. I also wrestle with them, play football, basketball, paint ball, go running or biking with them, take them out to breakfast, play board games, go on walks, and periodically write them notes of encouragement.

Notice that I never mentioned TV. That is because it is a passive activity. When you are building and maintaining relationships, you must be active! I recommend you take a careful inventory of the amount of time you spend watching TV and movies, playing video games, and make plans to replace that time completely or at least by 50%. It will be the best decision you have ever made.

All quality, vibrant relationships require time, self-sacrifice, shared vision, common goals, and looking out for the needs of others. All these relationship-building techniques will transform your marriage and family life, but are also useful in your business pursuits as well. Everyone wants to feel loved, and everyone is a kid at heart and you know how kids spell love... T-I-M-E. Now that you have the steps, build your plan and get to work!

Contact Dan Roose:

www.nogreaterwealth.com
Dan@nogreaterwealth.com

Shondelle Solomon-Miles

Shondelle Solomon-Miles discovered her passion for fitness and body transformation upon graduating from Columbia University in 1996. Since then, it has been Shondelle's personal and professional mission to improve and transform lives via the vehicle of health and fitness. In 2006, years after graduating with her Masters in Sports Medicine from University of Miami, Shondelle established Synergize!, a multifaceted small-group personal training center specializing in body fat loss and weight management for adult men and women. She states, "I wanted to create an affordable and results-driven alternative to traditional health club and one-on-one personal training. I really wanted to help people get permanent, and not 'quick fix,' results, and most of all, have fun doing it." Shondelle resides in Hollywood, Florida with her husband and two young children.

Contact Shondelle Solomon-Miles:

www.SynergizeWeightLoss.com

The Five Core Principles of
Optimal Health and Physical Transformation
by Shondelle Solomon-Miles

A person on a mission to achieve their goals and live their dreams must make health a priority. After all, without good health and physical vitality, all the ambition, desire, opportunity, imagination and creativity in the world won't get you very far. I'm sure you would agree that your health is your most valuable asset and if it fails, you'll spend everything you have financially and emotionally to get it back. Despite this truth, health and fitness is one of the most neglected aspects of many peoples' lives. Family, relationships, career, finances, and a myriad of other life obligations often take precedence, and ironically so, because without optimal health, these other aspects of life are significantly compromised.

Today, we have more health clubs, diets, weight-loss centers, exercise protocols, nutritional supplements and fitness gurus than ever before, yet as a nation our health and fitness is declining, and the *majority* of our American population is overweight or obese. Poor diets and lack of exercise are a *big* part of the problem, but an even bigger issue is the pervasive mindset that equates health with the absence of disease. Thinking completely differently, a Visionary with GUTS knows that optimal health is not just being free of disease, *but being physically, emotionally, and spiritually able to maximize your potential, and to participate fully in whatever aspect of life you choose.*

That being said, I won't share with you the 'eat better and exercise more' rant typical of most discussions on living a fit and healthy life. It is my perception that the 'diet and exercise' conversation, although necessary, is the 'icing on the cake.' The problem is that many people are missing the 'cake'; the fundamental mindset that encourages better health, improved fitness and successful body transformation. In almost two decades as a fitness professional and body transformation coach, I have discovered five core principles; that when consistently implemented, will put you on the road toward optimal health and physical well-being.

Core Principle #1: Make Your Heath a True Priority
I think you would agree that most people would rank acquiring or maintaining good health as one of their top priorities in life. After all, most people do *intellectually* understand the importance of good health,

even if 'good health' is defined only by the absence of disease. Yet, statistically and visibly, there seems to be a discrepancy between our priorities and our actions when it comes to our fitness and physical well-being. Nearly two-thirds of our population is overweight or obese, and heart disease is the leading cause of death in the United States.

There is a difference between importance and priority. For example, in my life paying my bills on time is *important,* however feeding my children every day is *priority.* For me, drinking enough water every day is *important,* but working out at least four days a week is *priority.* Do you see the difference? Something that is 'important' *should* happen, while something that is priority *must* happen. Therefore, unless living a healthy lifestyle is considered priority rather than important, it is unlikely to become part of your daily lifestyle. This includes all aspects of a healthy lifestyle: regular exercise, proper nutrition, adequate water consumption, periodic detoxification, and stress management. Any goal that you say is a priority is only a *true* priority to the extent that you take action on it. In other words, if you say living a healthy and fit lifestyle is one of your top priorities, but you're a couch potato eating junk food every night, then you're fooling yourself. Life is busy. There are, and will always be, people, obligations and situations demanding things from you. However, the ONLY way you'll achieve optimal health and well-being is by considering it a priority rather than merely important.

Core Principle #2: Embrace Synergy

Synergize! is the name of my small-group personal training company. The name embraces a fundamental core principle of optimal health and physical transformation: synergy. Synergy occurs when multiple factors work together to produce a result that is greater than any one factor alone. For example, you could lose weight by changing your nutritional habits, or you could lose weight by being more physically active. However, when you implement a better diet *and* increased movement, your results will be greater than either one by itself. In order to achieve optimal health and physical transformation, it is wise to incorporate *a variety* of components in your fitness program. The Synergize! philosophy identifies five major habits necessary for body transformation and improved health and vitality. They include: mastering your mind, detoxifying your body, eating supportively, moving regularly and intensely, and managing stress. Each of these components make up what I've termed the Healthy Living Pyramid, and if any 'step' of the pyramid is missing, then you compromise the integrity of your 'pyramid.'

I know the healthiest eaters who refuse to exercise, and I know the most avid exercisers who eat poorly. I also know very fit individuals who are on blood pressure medication because they don't effectively manage their stress. Specifically within the arena of physical fitness, there are endurance runners who can't do five push-ups, and body builders who can't run around the block or touch their toes. I embrace the philosophy that optimal health and 'true' fitness is not about being extreme or even great at any one thing, but rather, the ability to embrace and implement the synergy of all facets of fitness.

Core Principle #3: See the Illusions of Perfection and the 'Quick Fix'

Lao Tzu said: "A journey of a thousand miles begins with a single step." Two of the biggest mistakes that I witness people make when endeavoring to attain optimal health and fitness is: 1) attempting to do 'too much too soon,' and 2) attempting to get it 'exactly right.'

It is the quest for perfection, and our obsession with the 'quick fix' that encourages this 'overnight-overhaul' approach. This is the mindset that says: I must exercise every day, or not at all or I must eat a 'perfect' diet, or not even bother trying. It's also the mentality that says: Why can't I lose 50 pounds in two months, or get six-pack abs in three weeks? Never mind the fact that it took you ten years to gain the 50 pounds, or your stomach hasn't been flat since high-school! Whatever happened to simply being better today than you were yesterday?

This search for perfection, undoubtedly influenced by popular culture, and the *illusion* that perfection can be found, is an inevitable path towards inaction, and ultimately failure. No one and no *thing* is perfect, and therefore no endeavor can be perfect. Some days will be better than others. Learn to compromise with perfection by striving for improvement.

The 'quick-fix' mentality will also derail you from achieving your goals. You live in a society that encourages immediate gratification: liposuction, the drive-thru, ATM machines and one-minute rice are all testimony to this truth. You want what you want and you want it yesterday. Instant gratification, my friend, is yet another illusion— and one that generally results in frustration and disappointment.

Instead of depending on the fallacies of perfection and

instantaneous results, I recommend choosing the health and/or fitness goal that is of top *priority*, and identify the behaviors you will need to change in order to realize this goal. Then, choose one or two small steps you can take *today* to move you closer to that goal. If your goal is to lose 50 pounds, and you need to stop drinking soda *every* day to realize this goal, then focus only on decreasing your soda consumption. The bottom line is: **Your lifestyle won't change overnight. Don't expect to go from burgers to brown rice, or TV-watching marathons to daily spinning class in the blink of an eye.** The key is to be conscious of the changes you need to make and take small steps every day to implement those changes in your life. Founder and president of the Children's Defense Fund, Marian Wright Edelman said it best: **"You're not obligated to win. You're obligated to keep trying to do the best you can every day."**

Core Principle #4: Get Comfortable with Being Uncomfortable
Nothing disappoints me more than when clients quit my training program because they claim "it is too hard." Too hard? Are you kidding me? If changing and getting fit and healthy were easy, two-thirds of our population would NOT be overweight or obese. When has anything in life that is worthwhile, and worth 'fighting' for, been easy? Nine months of pregnancy?...HARD...Giving birth?...HARD...Raising kids?...HARD...Advancing in your career?...HARD...Earning a college or graduate degree?...HARD... A successful, healthy marriage?...HARD...Getting out of debt?...HARD...A successful business?...HARD.

The bottom line is this: Everything that *ultimately* gives you happiness and satisfaction in life has at some point been HARD.

The problem is that most people want results and progress *inside* of their comfort zone. Most people want the easy road to success. Most people are not *willing* to pay the price for positive change, but are willing to complain about their lack of results. Most people are addicted to instant gratification and the 'quick fix.' However, it is those individuals who *know* that **NOTHING CHANGES,** inside **the comfort zone, who achieve the results. Yes,** you can choose the path of least resistance and optimal comfort. But, the problem is that *becoming comfortable with being uncomfortable* is required for achieving optimal health and fitness.

Core Principle #5: Persist!

There is one thing that a Visionary with GUTS would NEVER do when working to achieve any health and fitness goal, and that is QUIT! Unfortunately, quitting is far more the norm than the exception; for most people when trying to achieve their health and fitness goals. The reason people quit is that achieving goals is hard work, and requires discipline, dedication and sacrifice.

It's easy to eat 'right' for a week. It's easy to go to the gym every once in a while. It's easy to avoid sweets and processed foods for a couple of days. It's easy to pop a few pills, drink a few shakes, and maybe workout to an exercise tape a couple times a month. However, in order to achieve the lasting transformation and optimal health you desire, you must endure the long haul; you must persist. There really is no other way. The good news, however, is that if you make your health a priority, implement synergy, strive for progression rather than perfection, and get comfortable with discomfort, you cannot 'fail.' Inevitably, challenges will arise, but you will overcome them.

There are three ways I recommend to nurture persistence: 1) Want IT bad enough, 2) Focus on the reward rather than the process, and 3) Develop supportive habits rather than depend on unwavering motivation. Motivation gets you started, but habits keep you going.

I wish I could tell you that the road towards optimal health and wellness is one free of speed bumps, detours and even potholes, but I wouldn't be telling the truth. If you're seeking temporary results, investing in a 'quick fix' product or program might serve you well. However, if you want results that reflect the person you see when you look in the mirror, or when you close your eyes at night, hard work and persistent effort is the only way.

As with anything else, your results are directly dependent upon your commitment, discipline and determination; you will reap what you sow. The bottom line is this: It's not about whether you can transform your body and improve your health. Instead, it is about how long you'll persist in doing what you need to do in order to accomplish your goals. And when you achieve your goals, you'll not only be proud of yourself, all facets of your life will be positively affected. And you'll be an inspiration for others to follow.

Contact Shondelle Solomon-Miles:

www.SynergizeWeightLoss.com

Cecilia Matthews

Cecilia Matthews uncovered the power of our bodies to heal themselves through her own experience with challenging and chronic physical conditions.

Graduating with Honors with a Multi-Major degree, she now uses her true gifts and talents to easily help people and animals heal naturally and quickly.

As a Certified Health Coach with over 25 years of research in health, wellness, personal development and spiritual growth, she creates customized programs to help her clients get results. Cecilia's clients have the ability and the knowledge to take their health and healing to the next level.

Contact Cecilia Matthews:
Cecilia@jtsch.com
www.JourneytoSelfCareHealth.com

My Journey to "Self-Care" Health
by Cecilia Matthews

My journey to self-care health began during adolescence. I was born in Colombia. I was blessed to have been raised by extraordinary parents, who nurtured me with love and unconventional nutrition. My father was exposed to herbal medicine and natural healing before he got married, having lived with the Indians in Colombia for some time. He made sure that we ate the freshest and healthiest fruits and vegetables he could find in the open markets. Canned or processed foods were a sin to him and he called them "metallic" or "cardboard foods." Ice cream, sodas, and fatty foods were not part of our daily menu. He prepared teas and potions when we had colds and fevers. (I still use them today.) We grew up healthy, slender, and athletic. We joined him in walking and hiking, (his favorite activities), and at school, we played sports. We enjoyed a wonderful social life with relatives and friends. I also thank my father for sharing with me his obsession for **education and learning**, which have supported me during my journey to "self-care."

I came to the United States after high school and continued following my father's advice: **"Eat healthy, study and learn all you can."** My health and weight remained the same, so my life was worry-free. After finishing my studies, I moved to South Florida where I faced health challenges such as allergies, bronchitis, etc., since I was not used to living in a humid climate. I was advised to buy health insurance. Being by myself required me to play it safe, and being without insurance wasn't the smart thing to do. So, to protect myself in the event I got sick, I bought health insurance.

I quickly learned that just having health insurance wasn't enough. A trip to the emergency room for an animal bite and an ear infection proved to be very costly because the coverage was refused. Feeling frustrated and not really "protected," I cancelled my insurance, wondering if it was the right decision and whether I would be able to survive without it. A car accident followed, and I agreed to have arthroscopic surgery on my knee, convinced that I would be dancing in two weeks, as promised by my doctor. The surgery and the drugs together devastated both my body and my mind.

After a long lawsuit and therapy, which lasted over three years, my knee was worse than before the surgery. I decided it was up to me to heal my 30% disabled knee in order to go back to my 8-hour a day, stand-up job.

My mind was responsible for most of the healing. I simply refused to believe that there was something wrong with my knee. Searching for the best supplements became my focus and I tested hundreds of products and programs available to heal and improve my health and body.

Years later, I was offered an opportunity to work with breast cancer survivors. This led me **to confront my biggest fear in health: breast cancer.** Humbly I accepted. This was a great opportunity to learn and conquer this "demon." What I saw and experienced then would stay with me for the rest of my life. I finally got to see the two opposing sides of this giant: the financial side, versus the pain, suffering and mutilation to the women who underwent torturous treatments in order to survive the breast cancer. I can't describe in words the grotesque pictures.

I worked with hundreds of patients, traveling 100 miles per day, visiting and helping them restore their previous image before surgery. I will never forget them and am grateful to them for restoring and confirming my faith in healing naturally versus dying chemically. I learned how many women refused conventional treatments after suffering from severe side effects from chemotherapy, and from the inhumane treatment given by their so-called doctors. Those women took it upon themselves to find other paths of healing as well as other holistic approaches to diet and nutrition. At last, I had found what I was looking for: convincing testimonials from live and healthy cancer survivors, who I could identify with and learn from.

My universe shifted!! I made a **HUGE** decision then, armed with all this information. I declared that from that day on, I would do whatever I could to learn how to **prevent disease.** Since that time I don't fear the monster anymore and it is my passion to share this feeling with others, so they too can live free of the monster of fear of cancer.

What followed next put me completely in tune with myself and the health journey I had chosen. Diagnosed with ovarian tumors 10 years ago, I had decided against surgery, also rejecting the orders from the doctor to take medication. I knew this wasn't the "correct way" and that I had to again rely on natural ways of healing. How was I going to rid my body of these tumors? **I asked for divine intervention and I received**

it!! The gurus, the products and the programs I needed to follow, showed up, thus answering all the questions raised during all those years of research. The tumors faded away into eternity after a month of cleansing my entire system. The doctor documented this by performing a follow-up sonogram. While she was thrilled for me, she had no interest in learning how I was able to heal the tumors. That was my last visit to a medical doctor. Since that time, I no longer play "Russian Roulette" with my health.

My purpose in sharing this journey to self-care is to **convey a message** to **choose to commit** and take an **active and responsible role** in our own health and wellness, in order to benefit our bodies and our lives. It is not intended to indoctrinate, or change anybody's set beliefs or conditioning, but rather to inform those like me, who have no tolerance for drugs, that there's another way out.

This "Journey to Self-Care" is worthwhile and I feel FREE! I realize today, that the mainstream feeds us a diet of **fear, ignorance, dependence, and misinformation**. From the time we are born, we are led to believe by the limited and conditioned knowledge of our parents, by our cultural backgrounds, as well as by the government, the medical and pharmaceutical entities, and the media, that there is only one path to healing: through the standard medical and pharmaceutical solutions. In the past, we have had very little education, knowledge or power against these industrial giants. Fortunately, that can now change. **It is up to each one of us to decide who is really responsible** for the outcome of our health once we leave our parents. Our parents gave us what they knew and what was passed on to them from one generation to the next. We can continue **making excuses** for the way we treat our bodies, and **later pay the price** or we can take control of our health and well-being through self-care.

Yes, there is place for doctors in extreme circumstances. There is also a place for testing and diagnosing. But what about place for preventing and maintaining our bodies, like a car garage, where we take our vehicles for maintenance, oil changes and tune-ups? Seeking information and getting a little education is easy to pursue nowadays, with the great technology we have within our reach. We are the beneficiaries, after all.

Most illnesses and diseases are preventable by **US**! We don't catch or get cancer, arthritis, or diabetes. **We do** cancer, arthritis and diabetes, by ourselves, with our toxic thoughts, poor associations, unhealthy environments, poor eating habits, and lack of exercise and joy (in that order.) We don't need **medication,** we need more **education** starting at home, continuing in school and finishing at work. Remember that Western medicine is interested primarily in sickness and disease and not wellness. Often prevention is overlooked. Medicine doesn't prevent or heal any diseases, it only treats the symptoms and it forgets the causes.

Our health depends upon how much knowledge and wisdom we accumulate, the choices we make and the habits we develop and practice throughout our entire lives. I encourage those who have experienced similar consequences with drugs to join me in this "self-care" health journey I have been directed to take, so together we can climb the "Everest" of health. Health is a choice, and there is no price tag we can put on it. **"If we don't have our health, we have nothing."**

In this article I have only pointed out a few of the many instances where my health was at stake during my adult life. In addition to learning how to heal my body naturally, I discovered that the techniques I use also work for my pets!

This article is dedicated to the thousands of women who I've had the fortune and privilege to work with during the last 25 years. Thank you for everything you have contributed to my life on all levels of health, spirituality and wisdom. Your strength, courage, dedication and patience I will always celebrate. My full gratitude to Nancy Matthews and the Women's Prosperity Network for the honor of contributing to this project.

Contact Cecilia Matthews:
Cecilia@jtsch.com
www.JourneytoSelfCareHealth.com

Chapter 5

DO WHAT YOU LOVE, (GET REALLY, REALLY GOOD AT IT), AND THE MONEY WILL FOLLOW

"The success combination in business is: Do what you do better and do more of what you do." ~ David Joseph Schwartz

Introduction
by Nancy Matthews

The common phrase, "Do what you love and the money will follow" is incomplete. For example, I love to sing and despite how much I love to sing, no one has paid me to do so. If I want to get paid to sing, I must get really, really, really good at it. Take singing lessons, voice classes and commit to being the best singer I can be, which I have not done (*yet*). I also love working with people, writing, marketing and public speaking. I have taken classes, and workshops, hired coaches and continuously improved my talent in these areas and people DO pay me! Share your gifts and talents, increase your expertise and reap the rewards.

Being a "Visionary with Guts" will have you entering new domains, stepping outside of your comfort zone and provide the opportunity for continued growth and expansion. Whether it's overcoming stage fright (as I did), tackling social media or getting ready for your first TV interview, welcome each new experience with excitement and joy knowing that the more you learn, the more you earn!

Tammy Saltzman

Tammy spent 15 years in sales and marketing before going back to school to obtain her B.A. from Barry University, Miami, Florida and J.D. from Nova Southeastern University, Fort Lauderdale, Florida. At law school graduation, she was awarded the 1999 Outstanding Women of the Year Award by the National Association of Women Lawyers. Practicing real estate law for ten years, she built a large successful title company in South Florida. In 2008, she decided to reinvent herself and began a speaking career. Tammy compiled all the knowledge she had mastered over her career and developed workshops and seminars, designed to motivate others, encouraging them to harness their own inner abilities and successfully develop business relationships resulting in achieving the life of their dreams.

Contact Tammy Saltzman:
www.TammySaltzman.com

The 15 Second Reputation
by Tammy Saltzman

"Character is like a tree and reputation like its shadow. The shadow is what we think of it; the tree is the real thing." — Abraham Lincoln

What is a reputation? How do you get one or better yet, how does it get you? *Webster's New World Dictionary* defines the word reputation as: "estimation in which a person or thing is commonly held, whether favorable or not; character in the view of the public, the community." Building our reputation begins at birth. We are labeled immediately as content or fussy. As we grow, we continue to be labeled as happy, smart, angry, funny, reliable or difficult. Early in life, our personality is formed while our values and ethical principles of morality become established over time. Adjectives begin to emerge that reflect how others perceive us. Your reputation says a lot about how others interpret your character. In business, your reputation is the best marketing tool you have. One thing is for certain, it takes a lifetime to build a good reputation and fifteen seconds to destroy one.

Your reputation enters the room long before you arrive and stays long after you leave. Truly, it is what people are saying about you when you are not around. In the business arena, you will often hear reputation referred to as the "Corporate Brand." What are they saying? How is it that you show up in the world? Examine how your reputation affects you and impacts those around you. What opportunities may not have come your way because of your own reputation? The people in your business and personal life should be proud to be associated with you. In today's business climate, your entire reputation is only a click away on the Internet. Social media websites encourage full disclosure of all your intimate secrets. Please always remember that everything you post, all your testimonials, all your "friends and/or contacts" reflect on who you appear to be. Your personal image should be guarded carefully. Finally, first impressions always have been and always will be very important. My dear friend Vilia Kydd once said, "How you appear is how you shall be received." Always dress for success!

To reflect upon your reputation ask yourself these questions: Who am I in this world? How do I want others to view me? What is the true status of my relationships? Am I someone who can be counted upon? What do I value? What changes could I make to make me a better person, friend, partner, parent, boss etc.? If you are really feeling strong and determined to make some changes ask those around you for their feedback. Ask those closest to you for constructive criticism. I recommend they start with your good qualities and your strengths. Don't be defensive, instead take it all in, write it all down, try it on for a few days and decide whether or not it could be true. Then, decide if you want to make the change. There is always room for improvement in every aspect of our lives. Remember, the first step to change is determining what you want to change and declaring your desire to change it.

Integrity – this is probably the most influential of all four areas listed that can and will affect your reputation. Ethical principles and moral values reflect the type of integrity a person has. Honesty and sincerity are the cornerstones for integrity. Are you someone who tells the truth? Telling the truth all the time can be difficult at times. We sometimes make excuses that we are sparing someone's feelings or it's just a white lie. Once you make the decision to tell the truth always, no matter what, life just gets easier. Do you do the right thing? Helping those in need, offering help to a friend, holding the door open or giving up you seat for a senior citizen are all opportunities to do the right thing. Make it your mission to do one right thing a day for someone who least expects it. I promise it will feel good. Don't exaggerate and embellish, it's usually a sign of someone who has issues of insecurity. Finally, don't gossip. If you have nothing nice to say, say nothing.

Communication – there are courses taught in every college about communication. It comes in many different forms and it says a lot about a person. Are you someone who communicates clearly and effectively? When someone can clearly articulate their feelings, their communication is usually well received. Do you speak from "I feel," or "You did." The minute you say, 'you', the other person immediately goes on the defensive. When you communicate how you feel, the other person may not agree but they cannot negate the way you feel. Are you someone who loses their temper, and yells and screams when you try to communicate? Trying to communicate through angry intimidation will always destroy relationships and reputations. When you communicate, make sure that you're clear and have no hidden agenda. Finally, the best communicators are also excellent listeners. Pay attention when people speak and remember what they say. Listening is the one basic tool required for successful relationship development.

Commitment – I encourage everyone to under promise and over deliver. We often take on more than we can handle for all the right reasons but way too much at one time. Learn to say no! I promise, it is much better to politely decline a commitment, allowing someone else (and there is always someone else) to step up to the plate, than to over commit and not be able to give it your all. Are you someone who can be counted upon? Be someone who can be counted on to do what they say they are going to do. Do you complete projects and assignments on time? Don't procrastinate – if you need help or motivation, ask for it. Are you always double booking yourself and having to reschedule? Get a handle on your schedule; it's important to treat other people's schedules with respect. When you tell someone you will call them back in ten minutes, they are sitting there by the phone waiting for your return call. Don't say ten minutes unless you mean ten minutes.

Responsibility – talking about responsibility brings me back to the days of Werner Erhard and EST Training (now known as Landmark Education, The Forum). We spent an entire day going over their definition of responsibility and it literally changed my life. Being responsible means really getting that you are the cause of everything in your life. It's huge. Responsibility means owning up to your own mistakes and being willing to take the blame.

Being responsible means setting a good example, trusting your own inner voice and not falling victim to peer pressure. A responsible person is true to themselves. They also show up to work on time, never keep a friend waiting for lunch and are never late paying their bills.

We often need to evaluate our lives and the people we associate with to decide if we are being true to ourselves. If you determine you are not being true to yourself, then what are you going to do to change? It is never too late to change how we act in our lives or how we react to certain situations. Sometimes we may want to make some changes in our lives and find appropriate times to make resolutions, set certain goals or make promises to turn over a new leaf, and wipe the slate clean. So what steps can you take to reinvent your reputation?

1. Do an Internet search on yourself to see what is out there that other people may also have access to. Try to do damage control and remove anything that you can control;

2. Declare to yourself that you want to be more honest, reliable etc., and put a written plan in place to help you achieve that declaration;

3. Ask those close to you for constructive criticism, start with positives and strengths;

4. Work on one to two at a time. Don't get overwhelmed – take baby steps and make sure to acknowledge and celebrate each achievement;

5. Find an accountability partner – someone who can help you with your new commitment to make some positive changes;

6. Seek counseling when necessary. Understanding why you do certain things can often be enlightening and sometimes make changing easier;

7. Communicate to others your intention to change and ask for their support;

8. Do not over commit - learn to say no; and

9. Optional – make amends, apologize and clear the air with those people you may have disappointed. Often this could lead to a second chance.

Once you are able to take stock of the impression you are leaving with those you meet, you will then be able to implement necessary changes to better communicate the image you want perceived. If you do find out that your reputation is tarnished, I have outlined several ways for you to do damage control. It is never too late to change, and the sooner you identify areas in your character that need to be addressed, the sooner you will be able to set some goals for achieving the reputation you desire. Change always takes time, and actions will always speak louder than words. Make a commitment to change and improve, and be persistent. Slowly, you will start to reap the rewards of all of your efforts.

Contact Tammy Saltzman:
www.TammySaltzman.com

Trish Carr

Trish Carr is an International Speaker and Human Performance and Leadership Expert with over 25 years experience in Sales, Marketing, Customer Service, and Training and Co-founder of Women's Prosperity Network. As a consultant, coach and educator, she has worked with leaders and front-line employees in Fortune 500 Companies, professionals in the Information Technology, Medical, Legal, and Real Estate fields, as well as with individuals. Her workshops and coaching programs have helped hundreds of people influence others and achieve breakthrough results with powerful, positive presentations and captivating communication. To get your FREE article on the "3 P's of Powerful Presentations," go to www.TrishCarr.com

Contact Trish Carr:

www.WomensProsperityNetwork.com
www.TrishCarr.com

From Anxious to Awesome!
Presenting With Poise, Power & Confidence
by Trish Carr

It was the longest 5 minutes of my life. It was supposed to be no big deal, simply tell my co-workers about the upcoming picnic. I remember it like it was yesterday. As I moved toward the front of the room, I hear a voice in my head, "Wow, look at *all* those people," it says, "There's gotta be over 100 of them!" The closer I got to the front of the room, the harder my heart was pounding. "They're going to see that you're nervous," the voice says, "They're gonna have a field day with you!" Ooh…hard to breathe, hands shaking like a geriatric patient, heart pounding its way out of my chest. This was not just "butterflies," this was cardiac arrest. "Great," I thought, "First time talking in front of the room and I have a heart attack." Not a positive way to make a good first impression.

Fast-forward 10 years…My office phone rings, it's the Vice President of the multi-billion dollar company I work for. "Yes," I say, "I'm available for the next couple of days."

She goes on to ask, "Can you fly out at 5:30 tonight and do a presentation tomorrow morning?"

It was 1:30 PM. "Yes," I said, "I can do it."

"Great," she says. "You're going to be selling the corporate officers and their teams on the new online ordering system."

This time, that voice in my head said, "Ooh, what a great chance to move my project front and center. This'll be *fun!*"

This time, I was excited. This time, I was looking forward to it. This time, I knew that I would do an awesome job and that they would have no choice but to green-light the project. This time they would love me! Big difference from the first time I spoke in front of people about a simple picnic, afraid I was going to keel over. Oh, and this time, not only did I hit a home run with the presentation, they asked that I personally come back every quarter to give them regular updates!

The most effective executives, business owners, employees, entrepreneurs and individuals know that a key factor to success is the ability to influence others. To engage them, to enroll them, to inspire them to embrace your point of view. Whether it's inspiring your spouse to go out to dinner, or convincing your boss that you deserve a raise, we *need* other people to get what we want. The ability to articulate your idea, your message, your product or service is the key to getting everything you want in life. People who are good at influencing others easily attract success.

Do *you* want the life of your dreams? Do you want the chance to get *everything* you desire? Then presenting yourself, your ideas and your wants in a powerful positive way is essential.

Public speaking is a skill, whether you're in front of 1, 100 or 1,000, it's a skill. And skills are developed through process and practice. Whether you're sharing an idea, selling a product, or inspiring people to common goals, being able to present with impact is a skill that *will change your life*. And, it's a simple one at that. Really, it's simple. Remember, I said, "Simple," I didn't say it's *easy*. Nothing worthwhile ever is. Being a powerful influencer takes commitment, it takes time, and it takes guts. Yes, guts. Guts to move forward despite the fear, despite the "voices" telling you that you can't do it, that you're going to fail, that no one will listen.

In my workshops and coaching with individual clients, we build public speaking skills by focusing on the "3 P's of Powerful Presentations." Plan, Prepare, Practice. See, I told you, simple, right? Plan for your particular audience and your eventual outcome, Prepare your talk so that you resonate with and engage your audience, and finally, Practice, Practice, Practice.

Yet, despite building strong skills, those relentless voices in our heads continue to undermine our confidence. You may have heard about the study done several years ago reporting that the number one Human Fear is "Speaking in Front of a Group." People would rather be covered by crawling insects, be dead broke, or be physically ill, rather than speak in front of a group of people. Crazy right? By the way, Death was number eight on the fear list. Go figure.

OK, so it's totally normal to have butterflies before you go "on" in front of people. So how do you turn Anxious, Afraid and Apprehensive into Cool, Composed and Confident?
These 3 Secrets of Skillful, Savvy Speakers will help you turn that "nervous" energy into "excitement," and turn those negative thoughts into positive ones so that every time you publicly speak you are AWESOME:
  1) POWER YOUR BODY
Nervousness is Energy, energy moving through your body giving you

the adrenaline you need to be your best. You've heard of the "fight or flight" response. It's the response your body naturally creates in challenging situations so that you have either the power to face it and fight it, or the power to run away as fast as you can. That's all your body's doing when you're "nervous" before a presentation. It's adrenaline. It's energy looking for a way out. So help it dissipate by *using* your body. Whenever you feel nervous, whether its days before or minutes before, move around, shake your arms, stand up, jump up, punch the air. Add the power of your voice and as you punch the air and say, "I'm great, I'm great, I'm great." The more you move, the more you help your body create positive energy flow, giving you confidence and control.

If right before you speak, you don't have the luxury of flailing around because you're sitting in the audience or in front of the room, let your breath do the work for you. Your breath has the same power to move your body's energy. Breathe slowly, focus on it, see your breath moving through your body, enriching the energy and turning it into calm, cool, confidence. Breathe. Breathe. Breathe.

2)   POWER YOUR MIND

Oh, those voices in your head! They're going to tell you all sorts of things. Does that mean that what they're saying is true? Not always. How about choosing your thoughts? How about creating powerful positive empowering thoughts, rather than listening to the naysayers in your mind? Every time you hear a negative thought, simply say, "Thank you for your opinion," and replace it with a positive one. When you hear, "You're going to mess this up," replace that with, "I am an awesome presenter!" When you hear, "You're not prepared," replace that with, "I'm prepared and powerful!" Keep your thoughts positive and your presentation will follow.

3)   POWER YOUR FUTURE

How can you change your future today? How can you create a positive outcome before you even do it? See it, feel it and believe it *now.* Visualizing the positive outcome of any given situation, feeling the feelings you'll experience, and strongly focusing on success "fools" your mind into believing you've already accomplished it. Your brain experiences the visualization as if it really happened. Then, when you're preparing or thinking about your next presentation, your brain will remind you of the last time. And, the last time was a huge success. The last time felt great. The last time you rocked! Dr. Wayne Dyer says, "I'll believe it when I see it." See it now. Envisioning yourself giving the presentation you want to give, seeing your audience respond positively, feeling their appreciation and applause, gives you powerful ammunition against those "butterflies." So find a quiet place, breathe slowly, calm your mind and allow yourself to see yourself giving an awesome presentation!

The people most successful in business and in life are the people who can powerfully articulate their message to others. Learn this skill and you are on your way to creating the life of your dreams. Be sure to Plan, Prepare and Practice for every presentation. Power Your Body, Power Your Mind and Power Your Future and there will be no limits on what you can accomplish!

Contact Trish Carr:
www.WomensProsperityNetwork.com
www.TrishCarr.com

Burke Allen

Burke's Washington, DC based media, marketing and public relations firm www.allenmediastrategies.com specializes in helping folks just like you get on the radio, TV and into print. His clients have appeared on The Today Show, CNN, Fox News, The O'Reilly Factor, in The Los Angeles Times, The Wall Street Journal, and on dozens of local and national radio shows all across the USA including, Washington Times Radio, NPR, G. Gordon Liddy, Jim Bohannon, Coast to Coast AM, America Tonight, Mancow, WABC, KGO and many more. He also conducts in-studio media training workshops taught by national TV and radio hosts. For more information see www.publicityseminar.com.

Contact Burke Allen:
www.FreeMediaExpert.com

Becoming Semi-Famous
The Visionary, Gutsy Strategy to Media Mastery
by Burke Allen

It has been said that most of what shapes you into who you become happens when you're a kid. I guess it worked out that way for me, especially in terms of this whole "Semi-Famous" thing. Growing up in the coal fields of southern West Virginia, my thoughts were always on things bigger than my surroundings. I loved the stories of the comic book superheroes, especially Batman. Batman didn't have super powers; he just worked harder than the next guy. Plus, he had a really cool car. And, best of all, when he took the cape and cowl off, he was just an average, anonymous guy. Actually, he's a really rich average guy with a butler and a cute girlfriend. What's not to like?

I remember the day that Elvis died; it was a hot summer day in August of 1977. My mother, who'd been a fan since high school, was crestfallen. I sat in front of the television set watching all the coverage of "The King's" passing. I remember thinking about how sad it was that he was stuck behind the gates of Graceland. He never got to go out and have fun by himself. If Elvis wanted to ride a rollercoaster, he had to do it in the middle of the night when no one was around. Elvis had to rent out a whole theatre to see a movie in peace. That kind of life really looked like absolutely no fun to a boy used to running free in the West Virginia Mountains. And, when the big "E" died, they even had to exhume his body and move it back behind the protective gates of Graceland because of a plot to steal his body and hold it for ransom! Egads! I liked the Batman business plan much better. Go home, lose the costume and leave it all behind.

Not surprisingly, my parents were horrified when my very first "favorite" music group was KISS, the costumed, kabuki makeup wearing hard rockers. It made perfect sense to me. The music was best when played loud, the grown-ups were scared of it, and best of all, KISS was just like the comic book superheroes. They had the costumes, the cool nicknames and even secret identities! When Gene, Paul, Ace and Peter took off the makeup, no one had any idea who they were. They could go anywhere, do anything at any time and no one would bug 'em. Then, when it's time to rock, on goes the superhero identity and the costumes and away you all go to fight for truth, justice and rock 'n roll.

It's no wonder that I wound up on the radio before I even got to high school. It's the ultimate 'secret identity.' Not only did I get to be around music for a living, when you're on the air, you're the star. Everyone is listening, and they all want to hear what you have to say. You're just famous enough to get great tables at restaurants, free concert tickets and backstage passes, preview screenings of all the hot new movies and access to places and things that people with 'real' jobs can only dream about.

In my career, I've worked with and observed other people who've made an art out of being "Semi-Famous." These are folks that are close enough to being famous to enjoy the perks without having to deal with the crushing demands that real fame brings. And, I've worked with others who are REALLY FAMOUS and have seen firsthand what that brings. Being "Semi-Famous" is the way to go. Here are some examples:

You may not have heard of Jay Thomas, but you've seen him. Jay, like me, is a former radio personality. He hosted morning shows in Charlotte, Jacksonville, New York and Los Angeles before turning to acting. He's the guy who owned the pizza shop on *Mork and Mindy*. He was married to Carla on *Cheers*. He got *Murphy Brown* pregnant. He hosted the infamous *Who Wants To Marry A Millionaire?* fiasco with Darva Congers and Rick whats-his-name. Jay was even Richard Dreyfuss' best friend, the football coach in the great movie *Mr. Holland's Opus*. But, Jay can go anywhere, by himself, and nobody bugs him because he's not A REALLY BIG STAR.

My wife and I were in New Orleans staying in the French Quarter several years ago. I went to a business lunch and she hit the gym. When she came back to the room, Cristi said, "I just worked out with the nicest guy in the gym. He looked really familiar. We talked about radio. I told him you were in broadcasting. He said he used to be in radio too." Later, we found out it was Jay Thomas, by himself, hitting the exercise bike. I can't imagine Elvis doing that. Come to think of it, if he had hit the exercise bike a little bit more and the peanut butter and banana sandwiches a little less, things might've turned out differently. But, I digress.

Some years later, I was working with Jay Thomas and AMFM Radio on a project in New York City. Jay and I walked from the studios of his station right through Manhattan to Grand Central Station for lunch and to attend a press conference for Diana Ross. I was struck by how Jay could easily walk through the city, occasionally getting a quick glance, but for the most part, going completely unnoticed. By contrast, Diana Ross had to be ringed by security just to walk 50 feet from her limousine to the podium in Grand Central. People were pushing, shoving and making it impossible for Diana to even move like a normal person. Jay and I watched the press conference, he shouted out a smart-ass question to her about her hair style, and we went on to have lunch together in Grand Central without being bothered by a single person.

Here's another Semi-Famous example: I have a friend named Jim Brickman. You may have heard of Jim; he's a great singer/songwriter of romantic tunes. He tours, hosts a syndicated weekend radio show, has several Grammy nominations and has scored several #1 hits on the Billboard charts. Jim usually has someone else sing his songs, and he's scored hits with vocalists like Martina McBride, Colin Raye and Donny Osmond. Jim and Donny were even gracious enough to videotape a special greeting and performance of one of our favorite Jim Brickman songs, "Love Of My Life," for my wedding. Jim is "Semi-Famous." His fans know who is he is, but they're respectful of him, and he can move in the general public as he wishes.

Not so with Donny Osmond. I did an interview with Donny when I was with a radio station in Salt Lake City. Word got out in the building that Donny was there and every secretary in the high-rise flooded into the radio station. You should've seen the women pressed up against the studio window. As Donny and I looked out at them, I felt like we were in a fish bowl. What he'd hoped would be a 20-minute station visit turned into a two-hour ordeal of pictures, swooning and autographs. Donny completely missed dinner with his family. We finally had to have building security help him get outta there. Again, I say "Semi-Famous" is the way to go.

So, how can you become "Semi-Famous?" If you can develop a unique and compelling proposition that creates, or evokes emotion, people will line up to talk to you on radio, TV and in print, and customers will line up to pay for your expert advice.

Unique without compelling is useless, and vice-versa; if you are the only guy selling asparagus flavored chewing gum, that is certainly a unique idea. However, more than likely, it's gonna taste pretty darn bad and nobody is going to chew it. That uniqueness, the asparagus gum uniqueness, really gets you nowhere in this instance because it lacks...being compelling.

The flip side of the coin is this: you may have a great seafood restaurant in a coastal city with terrific food, but you're likely not alone. Most coastal cities have dozens of seafood joints; they serve everything from fancy seven course meals to fish 'n chips wrapped in newsprint. If you're just another seafood place, you've lost that uniqueness that you need to really prosper. So, no matter how compelling your seafood is, the consumer has nothing to differentiate you from all your competitors. As marketing pioneers Jack Trout and Al Ries have pointed out, "If you can't be first in a category, create a new category."

So, what is your business or product category? Are you first? If not, how can you differentiate yourself to become different from your competitors? What is it about you and what you do that's unique and compelling? Answer those questions, and you're on your way to becoming "Semi-Famous." I'll be watching and listening for you!

Contact Burke Allen:
www.FreeMediaExpert.com

Fiona Mary Ivancsik

Fiona Mary Ivancsik – The Exposure Strategist – "Your Online Exposure Strategist"

Fiona Mary has 18 years of experience in small business and is here to tell you a unique marketing strategy is vital in telling the world who you are; what you do and how you do it better!

As Your Online Exposure Strategist, Fiona Mary strategizes with you to harness the power of Web 2.0 and streaming video to establish pre-eminence and credibility in your marketplace.

Everyone is online or knows they should be. Now is the time to embrace innovative ways to market and the Internet offers this innovation. An online marketing strategy is a must! Blogging, Video and Social Networks are key to small business marketing in the 21st century.

Imagine a strategy to gain maximum exposure on the Internet! Imagine no more! "Stepping into Your Light Online" is the first step on your path to Online Success!

Contact Fiona Mary Ivancsik:

Phone: 61 2 9797 8951
Strategy@FionaMaryOnline.com
www.FionaMaryOnline.com

There are many ways to connect with me:
Facebook: www.FionaMaryOnFacebook.com
Twitter: www.FionaMaryOnTwitter.com
LinkedIn: www.FionaMaryOnLinkedIn.com
YouTube: www.FionaMaryOnYouTube.com
BlogTalk Radio: www.FionaMaryOnBlogTalkRadio.com

Stepping into Your Light Online!
by Fiona Mary Ivancsik

Online Exposure is no longer about having a website and waiting for traffic to come to you. These days, it's about reaching out and grabbing your audience by telling the world who you are, what you do and how you do it better.

You must step up and declare yourself an authority in what you love.

NOW is the time for you to be stepping into your light online!

Easier said than done? Actually, "it's Simple when You're shown how!!"

The Big Picture....What is Web 2.0?

The term **"Web 2.0"**commonly refers to the web applications in the period 2004 to the present which enable interactive information sharing and collaboration on Internet platforms, technologies and social interactions, such as media rich websites, social bookmarking sites, social networks, blogging sites, online forums and streaming video. A Web 2.0 site allows its users to interact with other users or to change website content, in contrast to non-interactive websites where visitors can only passively view information.

Web 2.0 users interact in a very personal way. They make friends, share ideas and develop communities. They access their favorite sites on a regular basis and play an active role in the way these sites and communities evolve.

The Web 2.0 online visitor has different expectations than visitors to traditional stores. They are more eager to buy online and they have noticeably changed the relationship between buyer and seller. They no longer want you to be the person selling and nothing more; they expect you to have a relationship with them. They want to feel they know you. This is why you need to be in conversation using Web 2.0.

What YOU need to know is that embracing and leveraging Web 2.0 is THE secret to your online exposure. To get people to come to you, you must use Web 2.0 sites, methods AND set up your own Web 2.0 site, which is where your Blog comes into play!!

The Web 2.0 Strategy
The Critical Factor-- Blogging

A blog is your Web 2.0 secret weapon. You need to be talking about what you love all over the Internet! Using self-hosted WordPress to create your blog is the secret to being in conversation online.

Think of blogging as the trunk of your marketing tree. Everything stems from there. Your blog is the center of your education-based marketing effort, and we know THIS is the most effective way of marketing today.

Your blog also speaks to your credibility as an expert. It is your opportunity to shine in your industry or niche. This is the credibility factor of blogging. Likewise, NOT having a blog is a big negative. One of the first things people look for when they visit a website is the blog, so be sure to have one and be sure it's updated often. An out-of-date blog loses effectiveness. An active blog keeps potential clients coming back for more information.

We also know that a blog is a strategic tool for Search Engine Optimization (SEO). Search engines love blogs because "effective" blogs represent new content, and that's what they want to give their searchers. Blog sites get SEO brownie points! A self-hosted WordPress site has MUCH higher SEO than other blogging platforms.

What's exciting is that if you don't have a website, your blog can BE your website. An "effective" blog is a simple, humanized, personal method to put up a website. Many of the websites you visit today are actually Blogs! If you *already* have a website, you can use your Blog to further engage your audience.

You do NOT have be overwhelmed about writing Blog content. It's simpler than you think, especially with the many content creation tools available and the ability to import Public Label Rights videos and articles based on the keyword phrases unique to your niche. Be sure to follow the rules closely.

Your blog posts only need to be two paragraphs, three times a week. Sit with a timer on a designated day and brainstorm topics from your business or industry. Chose five and write ten sentences about each. Voila!

Some effective ways to publicize your blog are to send it out to social bookmark sites, social media sites and even email it to your contact list. Social networks are another powerful strategy in leveraging Web 2.0 for your blog.

You can add your blog to Facebook, invite your friends to follow, and automatically feed it to post on Facebook. You can even put the Facebook widget onto your WordPress blog, so visitors can see how many followers it has. Posting your blog to your LinkedIn Profile is effective too. Currently there is no way to build a following among contacts, but it is another way to publicize your blog and adds to your credibility.

You can also tweet your blog posts to Twitter by installing a plug-in which tweets a link to your blog each time you create a new post. Plug-ins are one of the BEST aspects of a self-hosted WordPress blog. They are small software applications only available for use with a self-hosted WordPress blog. Blogger.com and Wordpress.com don't have this functionality.

You can also use your blog as your newsletter, feature other experts on your blog, to help you piggy-back on Google searches about them, and publish your blog on the Ezine Article Directory.

Social Networks to attract online traffic
Social networking is a big part of the people-powered communication revolution that will bring your audience to you. There are many social networking sites to choose from. What's important is that you choose those where your peers and best customers hang out. Always ensure that your presence is active and useful.

You can build larger, more diverse, and more valuable networks on the world's top social networking sites with the help of a service such as Open Networker. My LinkedIn contacts rose from 150 to 2,500 in 6-months, thanks to Open Networker.

My advice is to choose your top three to five social networks and maintain a quality profile and activity level on each. My personal choices are: Facebook, Twitter, LinkedIn and YouTube. If you try to cover any more networks you may end up a "Jack of all sites but the master of none!"

Your social network strategy is that all paths lead back to your blog. And your blog leads to your website. The tactic is to actively play in each of the Web 2.0 sandpits. After fun time together, invite friends and contacts back to your blog or website, where you will show them how you will "heal their pain." Then you sell it to them.

Video to engage online

This may come as a shock to you, but you've only got three seconds to tell your online visitor how your business is better than competitors.' The noise on the Internet is increasing by the minute, and attention spans are decreasing by the second. So you want your marketing to be compelling and provide instant engagement.

Video does this. It immediately engages, imparting your message.

Video doesn't have to be professionally done. In fact, quality will always be forgiven if the content is good and adds value. Be authentic and honest.

When you deliver your message with video you are positioning yourself as the expert. As soon as someone steps up and does something differently, he is perceived as an innovator AND an authority.

So what does this mean to you and your business? And how do you record the video, store it and leverage it in different ways online?

You can jumpstart your business and be reaching out to your audience with Video Email + Video Webinars + Video Conferencing + Video Online Newsletters + Media Rich Email Marketing Campaigns. All these tools empower you to attract, engage and succeed on the Internet with the strategic use of video.

The Internet Marketing System, Attain Response, will make this happen for you for as little as the cost of a sandwich per day. How powerful is that? Check it out in the Resource Box below.

Forums and Groups to build Authority online

Another way to build your profile as an authority in your area of expertise is to participate in forums and groups online.

This is a two-pronged approach:

1. Answer questions asked by members and contribute to discussions posted by members. Be sure your answers and contributions come from a place of service and give value. You will be rated highly within that forum/group. The rule is: no hard sells. Once you are seen to be of value, the members of the forum/group will approach you about your services or products.

2. Post questions and start discussions in such a way that participants' answers and contributions provide you with a segue to discuss your expertise, your products and services.

The success of this strategy lies in creating and building

relationships. The sales pitch is not made in the forum or group. Rather, you make friends by building a reputation as an expert in the forum/group and lead them to your blog/website to make the sale!

Join existing forums and groups or start you own!! For instance, you can join my groups and ask questions or post discussions. See the Resource Box below for links.

Blogging, social networking, streaming video, social bookmarking, forums and groups not only drive traffic and build relationships and credibility, they also make a big difference to your business. They enable you to establish yourself as an expert and step into your light on the Internet.

Let me know how you do with taking action and implementing these strategies to gain maximum exposure online. I look forward to it. Remember, it's simple when you're shown how... by Your Online Exposure Strategist, Fiona Mary.

Resource Box:
Attract, Engage & Succeed Online-
Build your Network with Open Networker www.budurl.com/OpenNet
The Internet Marketing System Attain Response-
www.TheExposureStrategist.com

Social Networks-
Facebook www.facebook.com
Twitter www.twitter.com
LinkedIn www.linkedin.com
YouTube www.youtube.com

Article Directories-
Ezine Article Directory www.ezinearticles.com
ArticlesBase Directory: www.articlesbase.com

Groups and Forums to assist with credibility & backlinks-
Forums- 'Google' for forums in your chosen niche. Example: 'beauty forums'
Yahoo Answers http://answers.yahoo.com
Yahoo Groups Australia- http://au.groups.yahoo.com/ and World
http://groups.yahoo.com/

Google Groups www.budurl.com/GoogleGroups

Fiona Mary's Groups and Forums to assist with credibility &
backlinks-
Meetup- The Internet Marketing Strategists Group
www.budurl.com/gq42
Meetup- Prosperity during Recession. Is it possible? Yes!!
www.budurl.com/g5s3
Facebook- The Exposure Strategist & You
www.budurl.com/la9y
Facebook- Internet Marketing Strategists Group
www.budurl.com/37c5
LinkedIn- Internet Marketing Strategists Group
www.budurl.com/wgum

Contact Fiona Mary Ivancsik:
Phone: 61 2 9797 8951
Strategy@FionaMaryOnline.com
www.FionaMaryOnline.com

There are many ways to connect with me:
Facebook: www.FionaMaryOnFacebook.com
Twitter: www.FionaMaryOnTwitter.com
LinkedIn: www.FionaMaryOnLinkedIn.com
YouTube: www.FionaMaryOnYouTube.com
BlogTalk Radio: www.FionaMaryOnBlogTalkRadio.com

Kathy Dedek

Kathy Dedek inspires business owners to use their imagination to create Power Point companies. She is the owner of Brilliant Technology Applied, and offers Customer Experience Management solutions to vertical markets. Under the direct mentorship of Michael E. Gerber, author of *The E-Myth* book series, Kathy and her business partner/husband, Bill Dedek are poised to take their background in technology and apply it to your industry. Brilliant Technology Applied has two products completed, www.bta4adjusters.com and www.bta4advisors.com, addressing the independent public insurance adjuster profession and chartered financial consultants/advisors, respectively.

Kathy is also the certified leader of the Miami Chapter of Women's Prosperity Network. You can reach Kathy at 954.727.0199 or go to www.kathydedek.com and download her free article on "Creating CASH for Your Business."

Contact Kathy Dedek:
www.KathyDedek.com
954.727.0199

No Substitute for Experience
by Kathy Orr Dedek

We have all witnessed poor customer service: the surly waiter, the indefinite call center hold, the unresponsive representative behind the counter. These time-robbing incompetents are sucking the life out of you. Don't you just want to scream, "Hey, Pay Attention to Me, Show Some Respect, Hello, I am the Customer!"

How many times has this happened to you? Why do so many companies make it so **difficult** to do business with them? Here's the most important question: "Is your company one of them?"

It is amazing what we will put up with. And when we get exceptional service, we think it is so out of the ordinary. It does not take much: a smile, a sympathetic ear, a returned phone call, action or acknowledgment of some sort on their part. But how can we make **our** service exceptional?

The Five Senses

One quality of exceptional companies is that they engage multiple senses. Take McDonalds for example. The store is clean, the employees are all dressed in uniforms; the smell of hamburgers and fries fills the air and, the person behind the counter asks, "How may I help you?" And above all, there is a consistency about it. Every visit is the same regardless of the location. You know how the food is going to taste; the service is predictable. The process is repeatable.

Is this how your company comes across? Are you appealing to your audience's five senses? What do customers see when they walk in? Is the office clear of clutter, the staff dressed neatly, or could the room use a new coat of paint or could your employees use a fashion shopping spree? Do you acknowledge customers immediately, even if there is a line? The visual appearance of your company has the most impact. This is the area that is noticed first and is the most memorable. Have you ever been to a restaurant where the tables were dirty, the bathrooms disgusting? Did you want to eat there?

Take a look around your office. Is the floor clean, the room bright, the entrance inviting, does the décor give the impression you want to promote? Does your website reflect the image you want to impart? Are you appropriately dressed for your industry?

The second most important sense is auditory. How are customers greeted when the phone rings? The most beautiful sound to someone is their own name. Make a habit of addressing people by name. When you put customers on hold, have music playing. Start using video emails to deliver personalized messages and use their name several times in all written correspondence. Think of new ways to incorporate audio and video into your customer's experience.

The third sense is touch or tactile involvement. What is the temperature of the room? Is the air still or circulating? Is the customer standing in a long line that does not seem to be moving? Are items easy to locate physically or online? How long does the purchase process take? Even if you are not the cheapest, if the buying procedure is relatively painless, the atmosphere pleasant, customers will happily pay for your goods and services, and more importantly, return for additional purchases. Consider Starbucks. People flock to Starbucks to purchase an over-priced cup of coffee. How can you improve your physical interactions with your customers?

Let's not forget about smell. The sense of smell is extremely powerful. Once I was traveling during the holidays. The hotel had a real Christmas tree in the lobby. Every time I walked through the lobby, the smell of fresh pine gave me that "I am home" feeling. This feeling was enhanced by the fact that the hotel was brand new, just opened, and the lobby was warm, a nice respite from the bitter cold outside and the clerk greeted me each time I came into the room. Four senses had been addressed. What a treat! Are you treating your customers by adding a sense of smell to their experience? Walk around and breathe in. What do you smell?

The final sense is taste. This does not always mean physically ingesting something. This is the taste you get in your mouth when doing business with someone. Consider The Ritz Carlton Hotel. When you stay there, they treat you like royalty. The philosophy at the Ritz is "setting the gold standard in hospitality." This belief exemplifies the anticipatory service provided by all staff members. What can you do to associate taste with your business? What taste do you leave in your customer's mouth after he does business with your company?

The Sixth Sense
All five senses (sight, sound, touch, smell and taste) combine to create

the customer experience. And the customer experience is not complete until you add the sixth sense, you know what I am talking about, that feeling in your gut. How do you make your customers **feel**? Do they get excited about doing business with you or do they hesitate to call because they think they are bothering you or you will be too busy to answer their questions? Are you sensitive to their needs or numb to their input?

The Magical World of Disney is the ultimate example of Customer Experience Management. From the moment you make your initial contact to well after your visit is over, the encounter is captivating, the service exceptional and the experience memorable. Turn your company into the next Disney. Apply the sixth sense approach to how you treat your customers and watch the experience quotient soar.

"I've learned that people will forget what you said, people will forget what you did, but people will never forget how you made them feel." Maya Angelou

Contact Kathy Dedek:
www.KathyDedek.com
954.727.0199

Chapter 6

WEALTH STRATEGIES

"There are a million ways to earn a million dollars." ~ Unknown

Introduction
by Nancy Matthews

I t's time to play the money game with you as the winner. The reason so many of us weren't winners at first is that no one told us the rules. It's time to pull back the curtain and share the wealth strategies and secrets used by all successful, wealthy people. What are they? Creating passive income, investment strategies, multiple streams of income, residual income, the power of leverage, and the power of giving. For years, these strategies were foreign to me. Growing up in a working class family, my parents didn't teach them to me (they didn't know them either). They didn't teach this in high school (or if they did, I missed it). When my eyes were finally opened to the truth of how money works, the possibilities to create wealth became limitless. Enjoy this chapter; soak it in and envision yourself playing the money game and being a big winner!

Loral Langemeier

Loral Langemeier is one of today's most dynamic and pioneering money experts. A *New York Times* bestselling author and a leading entrepreneurial speaker, Loral has spurred thousands of success stories around the world by giving them the simple tools to generate cash and build wealth. Born and raised on a farm in Nebraska, Loral Langemeier started from scratch. She created her first business at 17, and by 34, had established a multi-million-dollar portfolio. Loral has built a number of businesses in a variety of industries, including projects in real estate, green recycled glass, and online marketing firms - several of which have grossed millions.

As Founder and CEO of Live Out Loud, Loral has shared her proprietary strategies at seminars all over the world, teaching people her simple recipe for capitalizing on their skills and talents to make new money. She is author of 3 national best-selling books; *The Millionaire Maker*, *The Millionaire Maker's Guide to Wealth Cycle Investing* and *The Millionaire Maker's Guide to Creating a Cash Machine for Life*. Loral's just-released book *Put More Cash In Your Pocket* is headed to join the best-seller lists. In addition she has appeared frequently on CNN, CNBC, The Street TV, Fox News Channel, Fox Business Channel-America's Nightly Scoreboard, and The View. Loral has been featured in articles and/or interviewed in *USA Today*, *The Wall Street Journal* and *The New York Times*, and on the web at ABCNews.com, Forbes.com and as a regular on line contributor with the Huffington Post, The Bottom Line, Yahoo7Finance, and BusinessWeek.com. She has been featured on the Dr. Phil show as the money expert taking viewers from financial ruin to being able to create new money and build back their wealth. Loral hosts her own daily radio talk show, *The Loral Langemeier Show*, on the *Biz Radio Network*, talking with experts about how to grow and protect money and giving on-air mentoring to callers.

Loral Langemeier, CEO/Founder of Live Out Loud and best-selling author of the *Millionaire Maker* 3-book series and *Put More Cash In Your Pocket* www.liveoutloud.com

Train Your Brain to Gain
by Loral Langemeier

Most people are not born with the proverbial silver spoon in their mouths; the truth is very few experience that kind of luxury. Many people opt for settling with what they consider the average life -- you know the one – hold down a decent job working for "the man", buy a home and all the trimmings, raise a family, pay into a 401K and fall in and eventually (if you're lucky) out of debt. Does this sound familiar? Clinging to this type of holding pattern, people tend to struggle their entire lives making sacrifices and never really gaining ground. But, it doesn't have to be that way.

We all learn by collecting information, acting on that information and experiencing results. So, what we're going to think, feel and do in the future is based on results from our past. This is why people often keep finding themselves in the same old place wondering why nothing has changed. In order for the results to change, how you think, feel and act around money has to change.

In most cases, it's YOU who gets in your own way of a healthy financial life because you remain uneducated about how your money should function. And, that's not your fault. Most of us learned next to nothing, financially speaking, from the school system. Our education about money is primarily based on conversations and experiences growing up. We heard things like "Money doesn't grow on trees..." and that just taught us: *Money is hard to come by. You can't have everything you want.*

It is possible for you to adjust your views, and realign your relationship with how your money should function in your life and gain control of its purpose. It starts right here with YOU! It's time to eliminate the noise! I'm willing to bet you already know what I mean by this. Noise is comprised of those nasty mind monsters such as, confusion, excuses, procrastination, rationalizations, blame and distractions. Believe it or not, this noise has proclaimed mutiny on your brain and if you're among most people, it has taken over about 85% of your mental activity. *(Pardon the pun, but that's mind blowing!)* It's time to exercise your mind and build your solution based thinking muscles.

When you're confronted with an obstacle, what do you do? What are the first thoughts running through your mind? Is your first thought bringing you to a place of negativity? It's time to take control of those knee jerk reactions and **train your brain to gain!** Gain control of your thoughts, emotions, and ultimately your actions. It will take time and some effort, but it can be done. With practice, you will start to reduce the amount of noise going on upstairs and learn new, more powerful behaviors.

While you're learning to shut down that noise, take time to examine your life. How much of that noise has held you back? Determine where your beliefs originate and examine the validity of them. Most of your beliefs were formed in childhood, and carried through to adulthood. Your beliefs are reflected in your conversations about money, which reflect your relationship with money and, in turn, most likely reflects in your bank account.

Beliefs become ingrained in your subconscious, causing you to feel like you'll never get ahead, or that you're just not lucky, you're inadequate, or you don't deserve more, and you act accordingly without conscious consideration. You're often controlled by programmed messages about money and your potential. Most of those messages are antiquated and flat out wrong. Don't buy into them!

If you're not happy with the current state of your financial situation, you're in a rut. Part of your problem is running those old reflex conversations through your head. The point is to find a way to add to your income and use that money to live the way you want to live, build a stable financial future, and perhaps, if you're driven, to create wealth.

You don't have fixed potential, why accept a fixed income? So, if you're stuck somewhere between your current circumstances and your dream, start now to change your conversation.

Consider the following to get yourself back on track:
• Examine your current beliefs and that conversation in your head.
• Eliminate the noise that's holding you back.
• Gain positive beliefs and actions.
• Take charge and be in control.

So what do you think you could accomplish with a new thought pattern put into practice and a little reflection? A whole new life? You bet you can! There's an entrepreneur in us all. Many generations ago, it was thought that if you put in your time with your career you could retire and live off your Social Security. I'm sure I'm not the first one to say to you that this is a thing of the past. If you're banking on that, you're in for a real disappointment. It's time to adopt the behavior of an entrepreneur. It's what this country was built on and you can do it too!

My advice to you is… CREATE A CASH MACHINE™. Start a revenue generating business quickly using the skills and talents you already possess. By applying this principal you will have the ability to bring in $500 to $1,000 extra cash a month. And that's just to start.

A Cash Machine will not likely be your dream job but it will be your fastest path to cash. The good news is this is not a complicated process. You might find even considering the path of entrepreneurialism to be one of those times you have to STOP the NOISE. Take control and don't over think things.

Here's some food for thought when starting a Cash Machine

1. Keep it simple. Stick with what you know. Write out your skills and talents. It's the very best place to start.

2. Earn while you learn. It's not at all necessary to have a college degree in economics to be a business owner. There's no business plan or book that will ever prepare you to be successful. Just go do it! Cash Machines are based on what you know. What you don't know either learn or find someone to do that part for you. It's what I do!

3. Don't jump at every opportunity that comes your way. Find that one thing to develop that will get you on your fastest path to cash. Being scattered in your efforts is sure to lead to failure.

4. Create your 30-second talk track. This is also known as an "elevator speech." Most people talk and talk and talk about themselves. We don't care about you! We want to know what you have to offer us that will benefit us.

5. Test the waters and track results. Build a lean, mean machine. Make it tight. Don't overspend on the start up.

6. You can make money with no money. There are times in your life where you may hit a homerun with a venture, but right now, you need to concentrate on hitting singles. What's going to bring in consistent cash every day, every week, every month?

7. Don't fall in love with your idea. If your idea is not making money, dump it. If you fall in love with your idea, you won't know when to call it quits. Admit when it's not working and

ask yourself, "What's next?"

8. Being an entrepreneur is not 9 to 5, it's a lifestyle. If you want it, commit to it! In the beginning you'll want to eat, sleep and breathe your new venture.

9. Keep an open mind. If something is not "gelling," you need to look at new solutions even if it means getting out of your comfort zone.

10. Tell people what you're up to. Look to friends, family and past business associates for support!

11. And finally, find a successful business similar to your idea and model your Cash Machine after it! There's nothing new under the sun, my friend. Why not learn from others who are already doing it!

If you are serious about changing your financial future it's time you take control and take action. Creating wealth is like following a map to a destination, there are usually several paths to your target. It's not an exact science, but you've got to get on the road!

Take control of what you think. Start fresh with new ideas. Doing this will help you begin to have the right conversation about money and reap the rewards. New ideas create feelings of excitement and expectation that result in inspired actions. Inspired actions produce new results that close the gap between where you are and where you want to be.

If you're ready to take the next step in creating a Cash Machine, my new book *Put More Cash in Your Pocket* is filled with practical information on getting started. If you're interested in learning more visit me at Liveoutloud.com or pick up a copy of my latest title at Amazon or your favorite book store.

I wish you tremendous success.

Ready GO!

Contact Loral Langemeier:
www.LiveOutLoud.com

David Dweck

Based in South Florida, David Dweck is an active Real Estate investor, Realtor and a Mortgage Broker. His lending company **EZ Equity Loans** specializes in private loans for real estate investors. He has been involved in 1,000 transactions. In 1994, he founded the **Boca Real Estate Investment Club,** and has built the organization into one of the most respected investor associations in the United States.

He recently launched the **Foreclosure Express Bus** and hosts distressed bus tours throughout South Florida. He has spoken on a local and national level on real estate investing and has been quoted and written about in local and national media including: CNBC, Forbes, Wall Street Journal, and most recently, in Fortune Magazine.

For your free real estate investing report, visit www.bocarealestate.net. To learn more about David Dweck's Work Smarter Play Harder for Real Estate Investors, visit www.worksmarterplayharder.com.

Contact David Dweck:
www.WorkSmarterPlayHarder.com

Work Smarter, Play Harder For Real Estate Investors
by David Dweck

As a seasoned real estate professional who has survived South Florida's real estate storm, it is a privilege to share strategies and ideas to assist you with your real estate goals and endeavors. The real estate landscape is constantly changing. If you have trouble with change, I suggest you read *Who Moved My Cheese* by Spencer Johnson. There are many moving parts to real estate transactions. What keeps it exciting for me is that no two deals are ever the same, which makes it very dynamic and exciting. I am passionate about what I do and I thank you for letting me share that enthusiasm with you.

People frequently ask me how I'm doing, and here's my response: "Unbelievable… and getting better all the time!" You might think that's a crock; it's not. I have a positive attitude, on a daily basis; I am fully aware of what's going on around me, and I'm enjoying my journey through life. At the same time, I have endured the challenge of bad tenants, headache properties, and chasing borrowers who have defaulted on hard money loans.

The following are three of the top ten things every real estate investor must know critical to success:

1. Have a plan and stick to it!
If you fail to plan then you plan to fail. Period. This is some tough love starting here. What do you want to do? Have short-term cash flow? Passive income? Write down your action plan and your goals. If you are working with me as your coach or mentor, I assist you in formulating your action plan.

2. Have a team in place.
If you have a partner, have a partnership agreement; surround yourself with competent legal and accounting advisors. It is also good to have an "investor friendly" realtor, mortgage broker and title company. Have independent contractors of all trades at your disposal. Build relationships! More on that later…

3. Always, always, always have an exit strategy.
For instance, if you're buying to wholesale a property and you don't

wholesale it, be prepared to close on it and retail it. If it doesn't sell retail, be prepared to lease or lease option it. Have viable options!!! Don't buy on emotion; go with the facts!!

One of the most amazing aspects of the real estate business now is that it has perhaps never been a better time to buy. There is a very small window of time needing to be capitalized upon. If you have made it this far or if you are just starting out, it is important that you run lean and mean. Value your relationships, build them into incredibly strong bonds, and shred costs wherever you can. I love negotiating and I'll share with you my seven favorite words in negotiation: Is that the best you can do?

ACTION TIP: You make money when you buy. In addition to owning your own personal residence, commit to buying and holding one investment property that has positive cash flow, and you will ultimately own free and clear.

In business, trust, respect, and reputation are earned. Look around and see who has "been there, done that" for ten years or more and you'll see who the real players are.

Ask yourself these important questions to learn if you have earned a good reputation:
- How do I carry myself?
- Do I dress for success?
- Do I speak well in person and on the phone?
- Do I say what I'll do and do what I say?

I always put all my cards on the table. In fact, I'm so direct and brutally honest, I've more than likely offended some people along the way! While I don't mean to offend anyone by telling it like it is, I can feel confident that there will be no challenges later on, and I can avoid all kinds of headaches and maintain control of my deals.

I would like to share with you a few "Dweckisms" and other positive affirmations:
- Pleasant persistence wears down resistance.
- Real estate investing is not a spectator or speculator sport.
- At the end of the day, honesty and integrity go a long way.

In these challenging economic periods, real estate investors can remain positive and focus on working smart, and dedicating ourselves to being real estate entrepreneurs and housing providers.

ACTION TIP: Make lots of low-ball offers.

What is really important, especially during these challenging times, is adding value to your life and to the lives of others. What will be your legacy? What is your calling? Daredevil Developer Frank McKinney's legacy will be providing shelter for homeless people both here and abroad, as well as building extremely high-end spec homes.

Real estate investing is a privilege and as investors, it is our responsibility to be regarded positively and to utilize honorable business practices.

Get involved in a real estate investor association in your community, and be aware of local and regional issues that could affect you. I founded the Boca Real Estate Investment Club sixteen years ago, and it has been a driving force providing value to many people. Learn from your mistakes and from those of others. Don't sweat the small stuff! If you're just starting, jump on in! For those of you, who have been at it and have reached a plateau, try a new twist.

ACTION TIP: Avoid fear and the "paralysis of analysis."

Make adjustments. Keep your tools in the shed sharp. Remember that real estate is a people business, embrace technology that can help you get ahead, never stop learning, and remember the Dweckism "I am a winner not a whiner, I am a warrior; not a worrier." I wish you great success!

Contact David Dweck:

www.WorkSmarterPlayHarder.com

Jodi Rozental

Jodi Rozental was born in Philadelphia and moved to South Florida in the 1970's. She has been successful in creating a multi-faceted career encompassing her passions: music and business. Graduating college with a Fine Arts degree, she pursued her singing and subsidized her income as a court reporter until she discovered the world of sales and her innate ability in that arena. First, she built a door-to-door sales business and then discovered Network Marketing. She became very successful in the industry. Jodi is currently the owner of a global network marketing business in which she seeks out entrepreneurs looking for an opportunity, and helps them achieve the success they desire through training and development. When she is not being a businesswoman, she is singing in a local synagogue, entertaining at weddings and parties, and thrilling audiences with her one-woman show.

Contact Jodi Rozental:

Jodi@YourDreamTrain.com
(954) 608-7203
www.YourDreamTrain.com

The Greatest Profession of Them All …
If You Have What It Takes
by Jodi Rozental

Being a millionaire is something I've always known I would achieve; I just wasn't sure of the vehicle.

I have a Bachelor of Fine Arts Degree, with a passion for music, a G-d-given talent for singing and numerous opportunities within my profession to share that talent. I am eternally grateful and would not trade this blessing, and the fulfillment it provides for anything in the world. I just know that realizing my dreams of financial freedom are most likely not coming from this arena.

As a right-brained person, not only do I lean towards creativity and the arts, but also, I am extremely entrepreneurial. In my search for my wealth-building career, I found myself working over 80 hours a week selling long-distance phone service door-to-door to small business owners. Then I graduated to selling all kinds of business promotions in residential neighborhoods. I was up at 7:00 in the morning and finished at 10:00 at night. I wore business attire and sneakers so I could move quickly. **Every day**, I knocked on the doors of 150 houses, three times around the neighborhood, and like clockwork, sold exactly 10% -- 15 promotions – to make **$100** and ring the bell of success when I got back to the office. I wouldn't come back until I sold that 15th one. I remember one day my husband called me out in the field and said, "Honey, there is a hurricane coming!!"

And I said, "I know, but it's still a few hours away—I just have two more cards to drop!" Another time, I recall knocking on a man's door, and when he opened it and saw me he said, "Are you alone out here?"

And I said, "Yes, why?"

He said, "Let me give you a can of Mace – this is not a very good neighborhood."

I replied, "Oh, don't worry, I'll be out of here before dark, it's just that I have a goal and I'm really close to reaching it. By the way, thanks for the Mace!" And I didn't leave that neighborhood until I sold that 15th card!

I was one of the top producers because I did whatever I had to do to reach my goals and be successful. And even more than that, I was very effective at teaching others to do the same. It was extremely gratifying, not just reaching MY personal goals, but helping others to reach theirs, and at times, that was even a better reward! This work ethic got me promoted to my own office where I would meet with my own sales team which I led, trained and motivated. I would earn an override on all of their sales, and be able to start the process over again of creating new leaders like myself who would eventually break away and have THEIR own offices. From that growth, I would ultimately make my long-term residual income and subsequent fortune.

The plan was great and my dreams were big, but there was a problem. I was newly married and I never saw my husband. I had one day off a week to do everything—laundry, shopping, catching up, date night. Sound familiar? My life was completely out of balance. After two and a half years of working so hard to build my team and open my office, I decided that this wasn't the right path for me. Giving up the rest of my life just wasn't worth it. But, I still stayed focused on my dream of being financially free and making a difference in the world. It was time to look further, because I wasn't about to give up on my dream.

It was 1999 and as I was walking out the door, moving on from those two and a half incredibly valuable years, a friend blessed me by sharing the opportunity of Network Marketing. She told me that I could still make a profound difference in the lives of others, build a team and make my long-term residual income and subsequent fortune - even while I slept! To top it off, I could work part-or full-time AND, from the comfort of my own home! When I realized this was true, the love affair began and the rest, as they say, is history. I have had an extensive, multi-faceted, exciting, challenging, fascinating, personal-growth producing and wealth-building ten-year career in this amazing, one-of-a-kind industry. I have experienced the highest highs, and the lowest lows, and consider myself a seasoned leader.

It is important to understand that being in the industry of Network Marketing is a journey full of fun, challenges, money, relationships, but more than anything else, personal growth. If you're not willing to grow personally, then this industry is probably not for you. It has a learning curve like anything else -- sometimes two years, five years, maybe even ten years long, most of it learning about yourself: How do you manage your emotions? How do you deal with different personality types? How do you act or re-act when things don't go as planned? And the biggest question of all: How serious are you REALLY about achieving your goals and what are you willing to do to make that happen? I was blessed to learn from my parents one of the most important qualities of all. How to maintain a **positive attitude**, and how to pick myself up, dust myself off and keep on going – no matter what life throws my way. If this isn't a quality you possess, it's the very first one you'll want to work on and master. You have the power to do it.

So let's say you've mastered your attitude. Excellent! Here is my next suggestion - Do your due diligence:

- Find a company you believe in and a product you are passionate about.
- Find out if the company is debt-free and has a good corporate structure and compensation plan.
- Is the product timed right in the marketplace and is it consumable?
- Make sure there is good support and training.
- See that there is a system in place to ensure success for you and everyone on your team.

I can tell you that in ten years, I've been through a number of companies to finally find my home. It took a tremendous amount of courage, more than once, to realize I wasn't in the right place, that my integrity was being challenged, and that I needed to move on. There are many wonderful companies, opportunities and products to choose from. Take your time to find something that not only has the necessary business elements, but is something that speaks to you, that you can stand behind, and that will allow you to work with people you like, trust and respect. When the going gets tough, and you can be sure it will, you MUST have an unshakeable belief in what you are doing!

So you have a super attitude and you have found your company. Congratulations! Now, are you willing to do whatever it takes to be successful and reach your goals? Let's get one thing straight about Network Marketing. If you think it's a walk in the park, you're wrong. If you think you "just need to find two people" and you'll be sitting pretty, you've been misinformed. If you don't really want to apply yourself all that much, then find another career. BUT, if you are willing to look at this industry as a respectable, viable, serious PROFESSION and you are willing to be trained, coached, and work hard for a few years, then you can be on "easy street" for the rest of your life.

So I ask you again, What are you willing to do? How badly do you want your dreams? Are you persistent, tenacious, ambitious and motivated? Do you possess staying power, perseverance and the ability to commit? Will you keep on going until you get what you rightfully deserve, or will you quit just before that happens? Network Marketing isn't for sissies. It is a simple business, but it is not easy.

Finally, it's time to take action. Set your goals, make your vision board, look at it every day, and then go to work. Talk to people. Know that more of them will say "No" than "Yes." Who cares? Every "No" gets you closer to a "Yes!" Keep sharing your story. You NEVER know who you're talking to or the difference you can make. But you MUST be in action!

What I love about Network Marketing is the lifestyle it provides: fun, freedom, travel, residual income, control over my present and future, the ability to impact lives and the vehicle to realize my dreams. It is a wonderful way of life if you have what it takes. It is an adventurous journey and I would be very happy to guide you through yours. You're going to be *somewhere* in five years…you might as well be living your wildest dreams! Let me show you how.

Contact Jodi Rozental:

Jodi@YourDreamTrain.com
(954) 608-7203
www.YourDreamTrain.com

Tammy Saltzman

Tammy spent 15 years in sales and marketing before going back to school to obtain her B.A. from Barry University, Miami, Florida and J.D. from Nova Southeastern University, Fort Lauderdale, Florida. At law school graduation, she was awarded the 1999 Outstanding Women of the Year Award by the National Association of Women Lawyers. Practicing real estate law for ten years, she built a large successful title company in South Florida. In 2008, she decided to reinvent herself and began a speaking career. Tammy compiled all the knowledge she had mastered over her career and developed workshops and seminars, designed to motivate others, encouraging them to harness their own inner abilities and successfully develop business relationships resulting in achieving the life of their dreams.

Contact Tammy Saltzman:
www.TammySaltzman.com

The Power of Team
by Tammy Saltzman

"Teamwork is the ability to work together toward a common vision. The ability to direct individual accomplishments toward organizational objectives. It is the fuel that allows common people to attain uncommon results." - Dale Carnegie

There is no successful multi-millionaire who arrived at achievement alone. Just as it takes a village to raise a child, it takes a comprehensive team to build a multi-million dollar organization. Each individual has their own personal strengths and weaknesses. Successful leaders know how to identify their own strengths and then leverage their weaknesses in the strengths of others. Building the right team is necessary when you want to achieve something that you alone cannot possibly achieve. The power of team is so strong it can help ordinary people achieve unimaginable things.

A team is a group of people who are all focused on achieving a common goal. It is important that the common goal or objective be clearly defined. The team members should all have an understanding of the common goal and the purpose or reason for the goal. Each team member should be clear about the expectations of the team. More importantly, each team member should know what is expected of them, how their activities connect to the whole and what is expected of the other team members. This will help each team member know where they fit in relation to the other team members, what they need to contribute for the goal to be achieved and minimize potential conflicts. When the common goal, purpose, and expectations are understood by all members of the team, they can align with the purpose and collectively become committed to the common goal. This collective commitment among the team members will synchronize both individual and team performance.

Creating the right team will require self-evaluation. We have already determined that no one person can possibly be good at everything. Identifying your own strengths and weaknesses is the first step to determining whom you need on your team. I recommend that you start with your strengths first. What is it that you love doing? It could be that you excel at marketing, but really dislike bookkeeping. When you are able to identify what it is you love to do and excel at, that can then become your primary focus and your contribution to the team effort. Most business will need expertise in some of the following areas depending on the type and size of the business:

Management	Accounting
Operations	Customer Service
Sales	Marketing
Fulfillment	Human Resources

Many small business owners will often find that they wear the hats of many of these positions. For a business to grow it is important for the owner to determine what they do best and stay focused only in that one area. There comes a time in every business that one person cannot accomplish everything or their time might be better off spent doing something else. The need to create a team may begin with one person, but two people make a team. So now, we need to evaluate your weaknesses or areas of the business that you don't enjoy and then start to recruit your first team player. Keep in mind, if you are not ready to take in a partner or hire your first employee a great alternative is to create joint ventures or strategic alliances. These partnerships can be mutually beneficial to each participant and could ultimately lead to a profitable union.

Team players have several qualities that stand out from other applicants. Team players are collaborators and can easily build off the ideas of others. They often possess excellent relationship development skills and are very supportive of others. They communicate well and are good at listening to others. Good team players understand their own personal strengths are required to reach the common goal. They understand that their experiences, knowledge and opinions make a difference to the team. Team players appreciate and acknowledge the individual value each of the team members brings to the team. Many of these qualities will need to be nurtured continually throughout the team participation.

Team spirit comes from nurturing these qualities on a regular basis. The individual team members need to be reminded continually that they make a difference to the team and that each member's success contributes to the overall objective of the team. One member cannot succeed without the other member's equal success. Each member should celebrate the achievements of the other members of the team to encourage a healthy team spirit. When team members are empowered through their individual involvement and through the contributions of others, the team spirit will soar. The more involved they are, the more motivated they become and the more committed they are to the common goal. Regular team meetings, brainstorming and problem solving sessions, along with accountability reporting provides opportunities for all the members of the team to be creative and innovative. Involvement in all decision-making processes allows each team member to feel that they make a difference.

There are many team building exercises and games commonly used to help foster team spirit. These exercises are used often so that team members are required to encourage each other, completing certain exercises in an effort to succeed. The exercises motivate the team players to work together and encourage other members to use their own individual strengths. Many larger corporations have been known to plan weekend retreats for the sole purpose of engaging in these types of team building exercises and games. These types of exercises empower team members, building their collective abilities to resolve problems and find solutions when they work together. These successful behaviors can be applied to reach their common goal. A planned brainstorming session highlighting a team member's issue that needs to be resolved, would resemble a similar process they experienced when trying to solve the exercises and games. Solving the problem becomes a way for the team to collaborate together in an effort to help a fellow team member.

Acknowledgement of each progress made is important to maintain team spirit. Everyone on the team wants the recognition that without their individual contribution, the team would not have been able to reach the common goal. Acknowledgement lets the team member know that their efforts made a difference and it provides motivation to keep going. The best time to acknowledge a team member is during an accountability reporting session. Let the communication be loud, clear and publically displayed in front of the other team members. Nothing will feel as good as being in the spotlight for five minutes of fame.

Resolving team conflicts should be addressed as soon as possible. Nothing could be worse for team spirit when a conflict occurs and not addressed. The team members having the conflict would benefit from the collaboration of the other team members to help in the resolution. If the conflict is not resolved, resentment and bitterness will often develop. To maintain team spirit and motivation make conflict resolution a top priority. Your individual team members and the entire team as a whole will be grateful.

I am confident that everyone is capable of building the comprehensive team needed to achieve their goals. Once you are able to really take stock of your situation and make the decision to reach out and find the right team to help you get the job done, you will already be half way there. Whether you are creating a partnership, hiring an employee or looking for someone to create a joint venture or alliance with, remember to implement these suggestions so that you, too, will be recognized as a team player. The best motivation for others is to follow in your example. Lee Iacocca once said, "I've always found that the speed of the boss is the speed of the team."

Contact Tammy Saltzman:
www.TammySaltzman.com

Michael Poggi

Michael Poggi is a nationally recognized public speaker and professional investor, developer and author with nearly two decades of experience. Michael speaks about how to buy Real Estate in your IRA or old 401 k plan. He teaches people how to make their IRA self-directed in the true sense so you can use it for real estate. He teaches people how to make their IRA cash flow monthly tax free using real estate.

In addition, Michael is also the president and founder of The Millionaires Real Estate Investment group, based in Ft. Lauderdale, Florida. It is the largest commercial real estate group in the state of Florida, meeting on a monthly basis to network and partner on real estate ventures of all sizes. Michael's company specializes in many aspects of commercial real estate, vacant land, development projects, and foreclosed properties. The group also attracts top notch speakers from all around the country who are featured monthly to provide additional education to the group.

Michael is often a featured guest on the Money Talk radio shows. His company, Build Wealth with Land, LLC. is one of the largest land providers in the U.S., providing hundreds of vacant lots yearly to investors and builders.

Michael has bought and sold over 435 vacant lots and bank owned houses in the last 10 years tax free.

Michael speaks about both of the topics below.

HOW TO BUILD WEALTH TAX FREE AND CREATE MONTHLY CASH FLOW FROM REAL-ESTATE.

HOW TO BUY BANK OWNED PROPERTIES FOR PENNIES ON THE DOLLAR.

Contact Michael Poggi:

Info@TheMillionairesGroup.com
(954) 306-3586
www.TheMillionairesGroup.com

A System Approach to Vacant Land Investing
by Michael Poggi

"Buy land, they're not making it anymore." ~ Mark Twain

You may have heard land is a great investment. The quote above emphasizes this very point. If the human population is increasing and the supply of land remains constant, then the value of land is bound to increase over time due to the law of supply and demand. Most people think that when they invest in vacant land, they are committing to a long-term investment with the risk of losing money in a down market. However, land investments can return a profit much quicker than ten, fifteen or twenty years, as long as you, the investor follow proven basic principles. For instance, by purchasing land in fast growing areas and applying the principles mentioned later in this article, property will typically appreciate at a steady rate in a short amount of time without much downside risk.

Don't Get Caught in the Hype...
Many investors identify a solid land investment based upon the buying decisions of the masses. For example, if you receive a flyer advertising land for sale in a given state, you may ask yourself, "Why would I ever invest in that area?" You then receive the same flyer over, and over again, unbeknown to you that the prices in this area are consistently going up. A few years later, when someone "trustworthy" gives you a tip about where the next great land investment is located, you finally decide to react. Thus, based on the suggestions of inexperienced investors, you invest all of your hard-earned money in an area that now overpriced. This is the first mistake of most land investors – they buy on the hype of an area.

Follow a System...
There is a list of key principles that we have gathered over the years that should be applied when considering your next land investment; these principles should be the basis of your investment decision, thus creating a repeatable system approach to investing in vacant land.

The first principle is doing your research to locate the fastest growing areas throughout the country. Our research department at **Build Wealth with Land** works diligently to find the fastest growing areas throughout the United States. Furthermore, we have found that the best investments are not in just fast growing areas, but **resort communities** in fast growing areas. We comb the entire country and locate undervalued resort communities, or hidden gems, within the fastest growing areas in the country.

Why resort communities? Think of a resort community as a force of attraction, or a human magnet that attracts people to a given area because of the activities and lifestyle offered. For example, resort communities are surrounded by many beautiful lakes, rivers, and streams for boating, canoeing, and fishing. They offer pristine golf courses, picnic pavilions for gatherings, and scenic nature and hiking trails. Recreational centers are also on site with a myriad of amenities, such as, swimming pools, tennis courts, and basketball courts. Furthermore, resort communities provide an established infrastructure with pre-platted home sites and low taxes and association fees. Thus, resort communities create a destination for vacationers, retirees, and active families.

As John D. Rockefeller once said, "The major fortunes in America have been made in land."

The next strategy is to stick to less expensive interior lots. Never purchase expensive lots on the lake or golf course within a resort community. There are a number of reasons why this is important: First, even though living on a lake or golf course may be where most people want to live, these lots are not affordable for the majority of people. Less expensive lots are easier to sell off down the road. Let's say your $5K doubles to $10K. Selling a $10K lot is much easier than selling a $200K lot, because more people can afford the less expensive lot. If you purchase a piece of vacant land for $100K today, and you plan to sell it when it doubles to $200K, it will be far more difficult to find a buyer at that price than if you purchased a piece of land for $5K, and it doubles to $10K. It is quite logical that more people have $10K available to invest in land than $200K.

Second, we found from experience, high priced lots have a greater chance of decreasing in value. Less expensive lots, such as those between $5,000 and $20,000 have not seen a huge increase in price over time, and are less likely to decline in value in a down market. For instance, a $100K lot may have been driven up falsely by investors during a buying frenzy and could potentially drop in price in a short amount of time. A $5K lot does not have nearly as much false appreciation associated with it, so we have found the properties rarely decrease in price. This keeps your downside risk to breakeven. We have also found that less expensive lots appreciate faster than the more expensive lots. Typically, a $5K lot will double to $10K faster than a $100K lot will double to $200K.

Thus, purchasing vacant land with a high retail value is a more risky investment, because you are putting up more cash; it is harder to sell later on, and all of your money is invested in one lot instead of spread out between many low priced lots.

Always think of your money like an employee - you want your money to be out working for you (appreciation), and then you want it to return (less time on the market) so you can send it out to work again.

Create Headache Free Cash Flow with Vacant Land…
Next, create cash flow from your vacant land. This great exit strategy will help you to significantly build your land portfolio over the course of your investing career. How can this be done? When you have seen an acceptable amount of appreciation in your land, and you are comfortable selling it off at the current market value, offer your buyer terms on the purchase of your land. Become the bank and "hold paper" on the lot. By offering terms, you will differentiate yourself from those sellers who accept only cash buyers. Your buyer will give you an agreeable amount as a down payment, which could be as low as zero down. Then, you will finance the rest of the amount due at an interest rate as high as 12-13%, which is very good return when you figure in your appreciation. You then take the cash accumulated from the monthly payments to purchase more real estate and continue to grow your portfolio.

Tap into an Unrealized Source of Capital…
Finally, investors are utilizing their IRA accounts successfully to make this system work. Building a mutual fund of land, or diversifying your vacant land portfolio, is a great way to see steady returns in your IRA. Most people currently invest their IRA in stocks, bonds or mutual funds, while foregoing the benefits of real estate investments. Land not only has less of a downside risk than stocks, but also a greater return than mutual funds, bonds, or cash. While self-directed IRAs are a great vehicle to invest in real estate, they are not used often because their IRA trustees

erroneously tell many people that you cannot use the account to invest in real estate.

Many types of IRAs can be converted to self-directed accounts including: Traditional IRAs, Sep IRAs, Roth IRAs, 401(k)s, 403(b)s, Coverdell Education Savings (ESA), Qualified Annuities, Profit Sharing Plans, Money Purchase Plans, Government Eligible Deferred Compensation Plans, and Keogh Plans. The creation of a self-directed IRA enables you to choose from an array of investments, whether it be raw land, single-family homes, condominiums, or commercial real estate. A self-directed IRA is a savvy tool investors use to tap into an unrealized source of capital and take advantage of the IRA tax and asset protection benefits. Only a handful of administrators offer truly self-directed IRA accounts.

Remember the best investor is an informed investor. Do your research, follow a system and reap the rewards you can sow through a System Approach to Vacant Land Investing.

Contact Michael Poggi:
Info@TheMillionairesGroup.com
(954) 306-3586
www.TheMillionairesGroup.com

Christopher J. Cooper

With over 20 years experience developing and marketing multiple companies including insurance brokerage firms, recording studios and many others, Chris has developed an eye for perfection and mastered the art of relationship building. "The challenge of selling is learning how to connect with people, you connect you collect," Chris says.

His theory of becoming a partner, not just a vendor, is proven with the tremendous success of Virtual Media International, a multifaceted company that specializes in providing complete service packages including product development, graphics design, CD/DVD duplication, printing, logistical support and easy online product management solutions designed for the public speaker community.

Chris is highly regarded as an industry leader. His writings have been published in Speaker Magazine and he is the host of "the Road To Success," a weekly radio show designed to educate, motivate and stimulate business owners, entrepreneurs, CEO's and sales leaders.

Chris is an active pilot, boating enthusiast and avid biker. He has built both his professional and personal life to be very fulfilling on a foundation of morals and ethics, and continues to make strides in the public speaker industry.

Contact Chris Cooper:
www.VirtualMedia.cc

The 10-10-80 Principle
by Christopher J. Cooper

There is no greater **joy** than the gift of giving. The greatest gift is to give back to the One who gave us the gift of life.

I have been a business owner for over 20 years. My business ventures include recording studios, lawn services, valet parking companies, insurance brokerage firms, insurance agencies and fulfillment companies. I have also served in the ministry for over 15 years. During this time, I watched my personal wealth both increase greatly and decrease drastically. When I look at this trend and compare it to my tithe records, my business and personal wealth was at its greatest when I was **faithfully and consistently** tithing. Now wait a minute, why did I include **consistently** in the equation? **Faith** is the trust in God, while **consistency** is defined by the steadfast adherence to the same principles, course and form. How I like to define **consistency** is the exercise of your **Faith** daily so as to have abundance in all areas of your life.

By applying what I call the 10/10/80 principle in your life, your entire life, you will see a return on your voluntary giving back, or faith. This means tithing 10% of your first fruits or income, tithing 10% of your time, and the balance belongs to you.

Let's clear up a misconception in what people think about giving money to God, or in other words, to your place of worship. Church is a business and like any other business. It requires the finances to cover its overhead and day-to-day operational costs. This is where your first 10% goes. The church also needs people to operate in the many different positions and offices; this is your second 10%. The fact is, God does not need your money and your money does not purchase your blessing. It is your willingness to place God first and by faith, trust the lord God with **ALL** of your heart, with **ALL** of your mind and with **ALL** of your soul that secures your blessing. That means trusting that He is above and throughout your business, marriage, personal life and finances.

There is a catch to this though. As I stated, there is no greater JOY than the gift of giving. But we can void this whole transaction and miss a great return on our investment by not following the message that Jesus made from the mount in Matthew 6:2-4, "So when you give to the needy, do not announce it with trumpets, as the hypocrites do in the synagogues and on the streets, to be honored by men. I tell you the truth, they have received their reward in full. But when you give to the needy, do not let your left hand know what your right hand is doing, [4]so that your giving may be in secret. Then your Father, who sees what is done in secret, will reward you."

God has given us a test:

In Malachi 3:10 the Lord says, "Bring the whole tithe into the storehouse, that there may be food in my house. **Test me** in this," says the LORD Almighty, "and see if I will not throw open the floodgates of heaven and pour out so much blessing that you will not have room enough for it."

The book of Malachi was written over 2400 years ago, around 450 to 400 B.C. It is the only time the Lord asks us to test him and in an area we are so dependent upon: **MONEY**.

It says that by bringing our tithe, the whole tithe, that we will see an outpouring, a blessing beyond our own imagination. This is a test I have seen come true in so many people's lives, including my own. The testimonies are endless and the rewards have been great.

The interesting thing about Malachi is that his name means "My messenger," "My" being God's messenger. Now during the time in which Malachi received the word from God, the nation was going through devastating times due to drought and famine. The divorce rate was high and inter-marriage was increasing. The temples were being neglected while the leadership of the nation was ungodly. Does this not sound like the state of affairs we are in right now in our nation? But King Solomon, the wisest and wealthiest of all men, teaches us in Proverbs 3:9 to "Honor the LORD with your wealth, with the **first fruits** of all your crops." Advice like this, I would want to implement quickly and without hesitation, especially from one such as King Solomon who has had it all.

A tithe by definition means "the tenth part of agricultural produce or personal income set apart as an offering to God or for works of mercy, or the same amount regarded as an obligation or tax for the support of the church, priesthood, or the like." Here is another definition. "A tenth part of one's annual income contributed voluntarily or due as a tax, especially for the support of the clergy or church." The word **tithe** actually originated from the word tehuntha, which is formed from the cardinal numeral, tehun or ten.

What I like about the second definition of the word tithe is that it says "Voluntarily." That's a very powerful word when it comes to money, as we are "Voluntarily" or "By Faith" giving back to God as He commanded us. Now by taking this test in all areas of our lives, we should see abundant blessing or growth in our personal and business finances. But, what if we added something more to the tithe, like our time? Imagine how abundantly blessed we would be not only in our finances, but in our lives and relationships.

When I was consistently tithing or giving of the first fruits of my wealth, I saw the greatest return from the test God gives us. It was when I went weeks or even months without giving that I saw my finances dive.

There was another problem with this lack of consistency that I recently experienced. I figured, since I missed a few months in my giving of my first fruits, that I could catch up at the end of the year. Let me tell you, that was a big mistake, and for several reasons. One reason is that I placed trust in my own system first and God's second. The next is the disrespect I had towards God that I did not give my FIRST fruits when they came in. They were really second, third and fourth fruits. It was I who decided when I was going to give my tithe.

And finally, the reason I feel is most important and worth looking at closely: When you consistently exercise, you feel good about yourself. Your confidence level increases and your endurance improves. You feel you can take on the world and nothing can get in your way. You are happy, healthy and full of vitality. It is when you start missing your workout dates that you start to feel downhearted, weak, groggy and sluggish. Your self-confidence drops and you become more introverted as you begin to gain weight and lose your endurance. It was when I got out of my routine of tithing that I saw my finances drop. I also felt my self-confidence decrease. My relationships became stressed. I was rude and short. My equanimity faltered. My business seemed a drag and I dreaded going to work. Then something dawned on me: the blessing was not there. The outpouring slowed to a mere trickle.

Shame on me for not being **Faithfully Consistent** and **Consistently Faithful.**

The bottom line is this: you pay your bills on time each month to keep your creditors happy and your utilities on. Your eyes are on your credit report in fear of your score dropping and you seek advice from financial advisors and CPA's on how to keep your wealth and how to increase it. What if GOD turned your electric off; now where would you be? Start building your score in heaven and get advice from the one who has the power to open gates greater than the wall of China.

10/10/80 for 2010. This is your year and this is the word.

Contact Chris Cooper:

www.VirtualMedia.cc

Chapter 7

READY, SET, GO!

"You don't have to be great to start, but you do have to start to be great." ~ Joe Sabah

Introduction
by Nancy Matthews

One of the first pieces of advice I offer my clients when they begin a new endeavor is, "Tell everyone you know what you're doing and watch the opportunities magically appear." All too often people get stopped by the paralysis of analysis believing they have to be perfect before they get started. In actuality, when you start living your vision the universe conspires to move you in the direction of your goals and dreams; presenting you with opportunities to learn and grow, create alliances and build your vision. We've shared how to position yourself to recognize the opportunities, now it's time to position yourself so the opportunities recognize you.

Rick Iacona

Rick Iacona – "The Millionaire Connector"

As a business owner for 25 years in South Florida, Rick's success is attributed not only to his strong connection to his customers through his superior services, but by giving them value over and above his products and services. Rick has an innate ability and gift of connecting with others, identifying their needs and providing solutions. He is also an accomplished actor and children's entertainer as "Poppy the Penguin" in a live show and video series. He was also the Play-by-Play Internet TV announcer for the Stetson University Volley Ball Team and former Boca Raton Street Parade Santa. He served as an assistant director for Business Network International and is a Graduate of the Referral Institute. He is currently the head of Business Development for Independence Title of South Florida.

Contact Rick Iacona:
www.TheMillionaireConnector.com
Rick.Iacona@gmail.com

You're Special Just the Way You Are
by Rick Iacona, The Millionaire Connector

In the late nineties, I entertained preschoolers as a large seven-foot penguin with red feet called Poppy the Penguin. Many of our shows were in South Florida and Nashville, Tennessee. Poppy the Penguin had red feet - penguins don't have red feet but he was still special just the way he was. We would share with the children that they were special just the way they were, who they were, without pretending.

I also had a very successful business for 25 years in South Florida where I was able to do what I enjoyed, doing something special just the way I was. Just being Rick Iacona, connecting with my customers, not just with the services I rendered, but by giving them value above and beyond my services. There was a bond between us, a relationship.

I remember from an early age, in eighth grade at my grammar school in western New York that before class would start, I was selling cough drops in the middle of January, the winter season. Then I connected with all the girls in my class and had them make me cookies or cakes which I would sell. I'd keep half of the money for our class fund and donate the other half to a charity. From that point on I was always looking for ways to connect or help others find what they needed. It was a natural for me. Being "The Millionaire Connector," it is my passion to connect people with that next person they want to meet, that perfect resource to help them grow to the next level and sometimes, just give them that word of encouragement which will get them through the day. What's special about you the way you are? What is it that you truly "love" to do? What is that passion that sets you apart from everyone else? Use this passion and your uniqueness to connect with others.

Take that natural, comfortable, "I love what I do" passion and have fun with it...Be Yourself! I believe that I have something of awesome value to give to others and that is Me! Rick Iacona, Myself! The ultimate gift you have been given by God is your "SELF." Always recognize this great asset. Remember always, receive it, increase it and never stop believing in it!

When you meet new people, whether it's a prospective client, customer or if you're at a networking or social event, remember to take your "I'm special just the way I am" belief with you and let it shine.

Let's have fun with Networking!
For some, this is an easy and natural activity, a great way to market yourself and your business. For others, it's not so easy and in fact, it's downright uncomfortable. Here are some tips I use to make networking fun (and productive!).

Make a Game Out of Networking.
Have some fun with it. Give yourself points for your efforts, and make a goal to earn a certain number of points each week. For example, 2 Points when you RSVP for the event

- 2 Points for showing up
- 3 Points for asking the person in charge who would benefit by meeting you
- 10 Points for each person you introduce yourself to and start a relationship
- 15 Points for follow-up after the event, a phone call or sending a personal note
- 25 Points for connecting them with someone

Spend Your Time Wisely.
Ask your friends and business associates who attend networking events which ones would be the best use of your time. Be careful. Some events just attract people who have the belief that the one who hands out the most business cards WINS! The one who wins is actually the one who makes two to three "good" connections and creates new relationships. The one who often loses is the one who's collected stacks of business cards and there they sit on the top of their desk!

Always Dress for Success.
Remember, you only get one chance to make a first impression. When you're meeting someone for the first time, you want to make a good first impression. People do judge books by their covers and they do judge you by the way you appear – and smell. If you have just had coffee or a cigarette, make sure you carry mints. Again, those first moments are so crucial.

Bonus Tip – Always place your name tag on your right side. When you shake hands upon greeting, our eyes naturally move in that direction.

Working the Room.
Now the real fun starts! When you enter the event, you'll notice that

different groups are gathered. Most likely, there will be a few groups where there is loud laughing, or the voices are a little higher than the rest. Those are people who love to be at networking events. They are the ones who will be more than happy to connect you with others. Then you'll notice small groups of two or three people. These individuals may be a little harder to connect with, but persevere. They are likely the power centers at the event and the decision makers you want to connect with. In other words, they're the ones that can make it happen. Remember to share your "I am special" belief and attitude and you will easily be able to connect with them.

A word of caution – be wary of the networker who immediately slaps a business card in your palm and proceeds to tell you every detail and aspect of their business without stopping for a breath, let alone to find out a little about you. This person is clearly only interested in "closing a sale" and not in "opening a relationship."

Bonus Tip – Make Sure That Person Isn't You!

Networking is one of the most beneficial and profitable activities you can engage in and as with most endeavors, you get better with practice. Becoming a "Millionaire Connector" is easy when you learn to have fun with it!

Seven Simple Steps to Becoming a Millionaire Connector. (Hint – these work for me…every time!)

1. Meet each new acquaintance with a smile.
2. Introduce yourself using your first and last name.
3. Always start the conversation with a compliment.
4. Ask "Feel Good" questions. Bob Burg, Author of *The Go-Giver* and *Endless Referrals* suggests you use F-O-R-M questions as your guide when you meet someone:

> F-Family
> O-Occupation
> R-Recreation
> M-Message (what they deem important)

5. Asking the following question will separate you from everyone else at the event: "How can I know if someone I'm speaking to is a good prospect for you?" I promise they will get very excited and will be bubbling with excitement to share their answer with you. Be sure to listen carefully and if necessary, ask additional questions. Then, ask for their business card (at this point you

haven't yet shared your card), and explain to them that it's important to you that you connect them with the client they are searching for.

6. Create a goal to spend your time with no more than two or three people. This will give you the opportunity to get to know them better and we know that, as Bob Burg said, "People do business with people they know, like and trust." Make a game of this as well, and only bring three business cards with you to the event. While you only want to give out two or three cards, be sure to collect cards from others so you can control the tempo of developing relationships.

7. Last, but certainly not least, follow up with your new connections within two to three days. This will certainly set you apart from others. Less than 5% of people ever follow up!

These Seven Simple Steps to Becoming a Millionaire Connector are applicable to every form of networking, whether in business or social functions. It pays to network in person, not only to meet new people, but also to keep your vital communication skills sharp. Practice making friendly conversation. Even if no relationship develops with that person, he or she will likely remember you as a "nice guy/lady" and if asked about you at some point in the future, would gladly refer someone to you. If your schedule doesn't allow for many networking events, attend only those vital to your professional or business standing.

Bonus Tip – Be sure to make the most of chance and casual meetings that occur during the course of your normal workday by applying the Seven Simple Steps.

Always remember - "You Are Special, Just The Way You Are."

Contact Rick Iacona:
www.TheMillionaireConnector.com
Rick.Iacona@gmail.com

Karen Wright

Karen Ivy Wright has never let obstacles get in the way accomplishing of her goals. Born with dyslexia, she successfully earned a college degree at Clark University and is currently obtaining a Naturopathic Doctor degree at Clayton College of Natural Health. She lives by the motto of Henry Ford quoted frequently by her late swim coach Doug Stern: "If you think you can do a thing or think you can't do a thing, you're right."

Working at Citigroup, Karen was fortunate to work with Pat David who inspired people to create their own success.

Karen has two children, Alexander and Mara who bring her great joy in their successes. She has put together a "cocktail career" for herself enabling her to utilize her strengths while keeping her passions alive. Her actions inspire people to take chances and follow their dreams.

Contact Karen Wright:
CocktailCareers@verizon.net
www.CocktailCareers.com

Creating Your Competitive Advantage
by Karen Wright

I was not born with a competitive advantage; I created it by using an elevator speech to obtain entry into the health care industry. An elevator speech is a short, prepared verbal presentation which gets the recipient's attention immediately.

I arrived early to an interview, resumé in hand, and waited confidently outside the office while my resumé was being perused by the interviewer. My heart was racing with excitement. I knew this was my dream job. I was positive that there would be a favorable outcome at the end of the interview.

Finally, I was called into the office. I could barely sit down before the interviewer looked at me, resumé in hand, lowering it to the trash pail and said, "You have no experience that fits within this organization. I do not see how you can be a benefit to me."

I could have easily slithered away with my tail between my legs as I watched my resumé falling into the trash. Instead of leaving, I took a deep breath and calmly looked the person in the eye and recited my prepared elevator speech.

My elevator speech had been prepared and specifically designed to show this person that I was, in fact, the best person for the position, despite the fact that I had never worked in that particular field. How was I able to do this?

After college, I landed my first job at ABC News studying trends in political elections through exit polls. I learned to identify how geographical, socioeconomic, racial, gender and income factors played a role in election outcomes. It was at ABC where I discovered the true meaning of deadlines and accuracy. If you were late on a deadline, it meant that the news was not heard and another station would gain the competitive advantage. It was equally problematic for information to be inaccurate. Inaccuracy caused faulty information to be spread by people assuming that the news they saw was correct. There was no way to guarantee that the same population heard the correction. Misinformed decisions could be made because of the incorrect facts. Both missing deadlines and inaccuracy causes a news network to lose credibility. The skills I gained from this job were: identifying patterns, keeping deadlines and portraying accurate information, which are also essential to any health organization.

After six years at ABC, I decided it was time to learn a new skill. I went back to school to study computer programming in a curriculum designed for people with college degrees. I was a natural in programming and quickly landed a job after the program's completion. My skill in identifying patterns in election trends helped me to easily identify patterns in bits and bytes, which is necessary to be an efficient coder. Once again accuracy played an important role in my job. This time it meant the business could lose a lot of its revenue base. Each new computer language that came along meant studying again. I learned the languages of Assembler, COBOL, FORTRAN, C and Java effortlessly as if born inside a computer processor. My constant studying and application of what I learned showed that I could easily adapt and flourish in any situation.

After two decades in a successful computer programming career, I decided to go back to school and become a Naturopathic Doctor (ND) to fulfill my mission of educating people about their bodies through a collaborative approach between the client and myself. This collaboration would explore the different available options to improve the person's overall physical well-being. I was now learning about the most sophisticated processor, the human body. I enrolled in a challenging program at Clayton College of Natural Health, a structured and well-crafted program. I joined groups that were health-related, attended conferences in the field and read books in addition to my coursework. The more I read, the more I wanted to work in the field. An opportunity to work in the health field occurred during my studies. This opportunity required me to take a detour with different training before completing the ND program. It would provide me with practical experience in the health field before I had an ND degree. I landed an interview with a non-profit detoxification organization that would pay for this training.

Here, I was sitting across from the interviewer watching my resumé fall into the trash and I was ready with my elevator speech. I explained how all my career choices prepared me to do this job. In my first job, I identified patterns in politics and learned about the importance of accuracy and deadlines. In my next career, I learned to identify patterns in order to create more efficient business processes. This new position would allow me to use the skills I had acquired to find patterns in the human body. It is essential to be accurate and meet all deadlines when working with people in a health capacity. I had gained these skills throughout my career. All my different career paths required the same skill sets. They just used a different medium. Therefore, I am the perfect candidate for this job. I had turned the whole interview around. By the time I left, the interviewer had offered me the necessary training to be a detoxification specialist and a job in the detoxification project upon completing the training.

What got me the position was the ability to identify the link between all my career paths and to incorporate it into my elevator speech. Since all my experiences were in different areas, I needed to show a strong relationship between each career and the skills required to obtain the current position. Without doing that, I would not have had a successful outcome at the end of the interview.

To move toward your goal, you have to be willing to take risks and be prepared for failure. At the end of the interview, my resumé could have stayed in the garbage. This was a strong possibility since I entered the process without any experience in the health industry. However, I knew that this is what I wanted, and was I willing to take that risk. If I failed, I could always try again. When changing careers to a different field, do not listen to the noise of other people telling you it cannot be done; you're too old; or you won't be able to succeed. If you are passionate about what you want to do, you will succeed.

The best piece of advice that I can give before returning to my ND studies is for you to study. If you want to be a successful businessperson, study the habits of a successful business person; a successful lawyer, study a successful lawyer; successful programmer, study the newest programming language. And if you want to work in a foreign country, study that country's culture and language. The key point here is that studying what you are most passionate about accomplishing will lead to success. On that note, I must get back to my studies.

Contact Karen Wright:

CocktailCareers@verizon.net
www.CocktailCareers.com

Oreet Mizrahi, AICI

Oreet is a Body Image and Appearance Expert, with profound understanding of the principles of proportion, style, wardrobe and body awareness. It is easy to understand how Oreet earned a rapid reputation worldwide. Although Oreet is familiar with many aspects of image consultancy, her passion lies with non-verbal communication and body perception.

Specializing in the areas of semiotic: signs and symbols in non verbal communication, Oreet is an International Certified Image Consultant who is also a certified Self-Esteem Coach. Oreet deems that the most-important "good first impression" coupled with a commanding, constant presence is definitely the key to personal and professional success. Residing in Parkland, Florida with her husband, Yoel, and their four children, Oreet has a goal to live life with passion!

Expressing Excellence, Confidence & Style

Contact Oreet Mizrahi:
(561)789-1313
oreet@mizrahiimage.com
www.mizrahiimage.com

Image Power Magic
The Secret Behind Every Success Story
Create, Enhance and Promote Your Best Image and Live
the Life of Your Dreams
by Oreet Mizrahi, AICI

You've seen this person before. How can you ever forget! You've always wanted to be this person. You, too, want to look the part, achieve ultimate success and attract wealth and joy into your life. You have been constantly trying to be in control and live your life to the fullest. You vision yourself entering a room full of people. You, too, want to look confident, be smiling, engaging and engaged. You want to attract the attention you deserve and to contract your real worth value. But, you are not! Why aren't you? What is it that you have been missing? What is it that you are not doing right?

I want to ask you to take a good, hard look at your life at this moment. What is it that you really want to be? Where do you want to go? What kind of life do you really want to live? Take a moment, and look at yourself in a full-length mirror. Be open and sincere, and just study your reflection. Try to see yourself as others see you. Ask yourself whom you're really seeing.

The Image you project to the world is a very powerful tool on your way to success. It plays an important part in shaping people's opinion of you and of how you feel about yourself. Modern life is fast. Contacts are quick and often you only have one chance to tell people who you are. You cannot afford to send the wrong message. The right image that you fail to project, might very well be the missing piece to your way to success. The right image will provide the lifestyle change you have been dreaming of and will change your life forever. A polished refined image has the ability to implant beliefs, motivation and inspiration. It can also provide support in conquering fears that may have held you back. Once you feel good about the way you look, your self-esteem and self-confidence will increase dramatically. Chances of career advancement will develop significantly. You will walk, talk and think differently. Business and social relationships will blossom. Doors will magically open for you and you will attract new and exciting opportunities. This will cause others to recognize and respond to you in a positive way. Now, doesn't that sound just like what you've always wanted?

So, how do you build an image that reflects the message you want to convey and give you an advantage in both your personal and professional life?

According to psychologist, Albert Mehrabian, your appearance and body language account for 55% of the impression you make. Your voice accounts for 38% and the words you use only 7%. Please note, your personal image has nothing to do with your age, shape, weight or beauty. You don't need to look a certain way in order to achieve a better personal image. All you need to do is to be aware of your image, know how to enhance it, and unleash your image power magic.

3 Steps to Unleash Your Image Power Magic
To make your image work for you, you must Dress Your Vision, Talk Your Vision, and Walk Your Vision! You should be the walking, talking prime example of proud and successful!

1. Dress Your Vision – The Power of Your Clothing Statement
The clothes you wear is the person you become. In which direction do you want to move? Are you ready to face success and be a winner? What you wear affects your mode and acts. Have you noticed the change in the way you do something when you are dressed in a certain way? Try talking in front of a group of people. Note the change in your feelings, tone, and movements when delivering your speech while dressed professionally and appropriately. Now, imagine yourself delivering the same speech but this time dressed in a shabby worn out clothes. What a difference! The easiest and quickest way to change your life and move through success is to dress yourself according to the vision you have in mind. Clothes have the power to create an illusion. Whatever role you play the most is the person you tend to become.

You can choose the qualities you want to project and the role you want to play. Decide what kind of person you want to be. Envision the life you want to live. Picture the sort of person you want to become. Go ahead; invent yourself. Let your imagination run free. Add as many details to your vision as possible. See it, feel it, hear it. Now, translate your thoughts and fantasies into action. Choose to dress according to your vision. Before you know it, you will become your vision and your dream will become your reality. The person you have invented will become you, and the life you have been dreaming of will become your reality. By choosing to dress according to your dream, you make your thoughts visible and really translate your fantasizes into action. Don't miss out on your dreams. Dress up your fantasy. Put on clothes in line with your vision and let clothes lead you to success.

2. Talk Your Vision – Grooming to Success!
Nothing announces success more than a clean, well groomed appearance. Appearance matters and part of looking good and sending positive information about you is maintaining a clean and fresh look. Grooming speaks volumes about you. When you show that you take care of yourself, it sends the message that you respect yourself and that you respect others. A neat appearance shows others that as much as you value yourself, you also value the people around you. It shows that you have made the effort to be pleasing to others. A well maintained and groomed look also sends the message that you are fit, well and vigorous. The image you project is of an energetic, vital person and people would want to engage with you. Your appearance will attract people to you and will make them give you the attention you deserve. Well maintained appearance includes taking care of hair (including facial hair for both men and women), skin, and nails. It also includes taking care of body odors. Make sure your breath is fresh and that your body has a pleasant smell. Nothing kills your chance to make it and do well than an unpleasant smell. Open the door to your success by keeping neat and fresh.

3. Walk Your Vision – The Alphabets of Body Language
Body Language is a key element in communication. The way you carry yourself and the way you move your body has a great impact on how you look and feel and what others think of you. Just by changing your body language you can immediately feel better, look amazing and make people see you and treat you as significant. Developing awareness of your own body language will help you in both business and social interactions and will increase your self-esteem. When you know exactly which postures, gestures, and movements create trust, respect, and influence, you can convey powerful messages. A fine physical presentation consists of exhibiting good posture, expressing natural grace and maintaining direct

eye contact. Your handshake must be firm and your facial expressions need to be pleasant and relaxed. Most important, smile, smile, smile! A genuine, sincere smile will change your world! Smile and witness the miracles revolving your way. Speak body language cues and send signals of what you want to be and how you want to be perceived and this is what you will become. Move your body in a way that declares success and you will become successful. Choose what you want to be and carry yourself as such. "Speak" body language of confidence and assurance and this is what you will pull toward you. You will feel empowered and blessings and abundance will be coming into your life.

"When your image improves, your performance improves. If you don't like who you are and where you are, don't worry about it because you're not stuck either with who you are or where you are. You can grow. You can change. You can be more than you are." ~ Zig Ziglar

You are now equipped with the knowledge and information to create, market and promote your best personal image. If in doubt, hire a professional. Consider hiring an image consultant, a personal branding coach, or an executive coach to work with you and help you put together your best possible personal image. Now that you know what impact your personal image can have on you and how it can shape your life, you can no longer afford to ignore its power. Your improved image can clearly take you on a journey to a full, more productive and successful life.

Master your image power, and use it for your advantage. Make your life a masterpiece. Change your life for the better. Create your best image and be who you were meant to be. Let your image power get you what you want to get from life and to make your dreams come true. Start from the outside and work your way to a successful strong inside. Look the part, become the part, be successful! Start mastering your personal image power today!

"Success means having the courage, the determination and the will to become the person you believe you were meant to be." ~George Sheehan

Contact Oreet Mizrahi:
(561)789-1313
oreet@mizrahiimage.com
www.mizrahiimage.com

Chapter 8

KEEPING YOUR DREAM ALIVE

"There's no scarcity of opportunity to make a living at what you love. There is only a scarcity of resolve to make it happen."
~ Wayne Dyer

Introduction
by Nancy Matthews

Keeping your dream alive is quite simple really, it may not be easy, but it's simple. If it was easy, everyone would be doing it. I know you have what it takes. I know you want what it brings. Freedom, joy and fulfillment. The freedom to create each day from a space of excitement and anticipation of wonderful miracles. Freedom to travel, to give to others, to splurge and enjoy the fruits of your labor. Joy in expressing the highest version of yourself. Fulfillment in sharing your gifts and talents with others and knowing you made a difference. Keeping your dream alive is simple and it's up to you do it. You have the power, the desire and the resources. Your persistence, commitment and faith will bring the magical results of living the life of your dreams

John Di Lemme

In September 2001, John Di Lemme founded Di Lemme Development Group, Inc., a company known worldwide for its role in expanding the personal development industry. As president and CEO, John strives for excellence in every area of his business and believes that you must surround yourself with a like-minded team in order to stay on top of your game.

In addition to building a successful company, John has changed lives around the globe as an international motivational speaker that has spoken in over five hundred venues. Over the past ten years, he has shared the stage with the best of the best including Dr. John Maxwell, Dennis Waitley, Jim Rohn, Les Brown, Mark Victor Hansen and Loral Langemeier only to name a few. This is truly an amazing feat for someone that was clinically diagnosed as a stutterer at a very young age and told that he would never speak fluently.

John truly believes that everyone needs personal development to reach their full potential in life, and his determination to reach all forms of media with his motivational messages has catapulted his career. John has produced over two hundred fifty products and is an accomplished author of seven books including his latest best selling book, "10 Life Lessons on How to Find Your Why Now & Achieve Ultimate Success." John has also been featured on many television programs and interviewed countless times. As a multi-million dollar entrepreneur, John is one of the most highly sought after strategic business coaches in the world.

John's passion is to teach others how to live a champion life despite the label that society has placed on them. Through his books, audio/video materials, sold-out live seminars, numerous television interviews, intensive training boot camps, live webinars, website (www.ChampionsLiveFree.com), podcasts and weekly tele-classes, John

How to Build Champion Habits
by John Di Lemme

Our habits, good or bad, are developed over our lifetime. They reflect the things we believe, the things we read and listen to, and our choices in friends. Our lives are defined by our habits.

Every habit you possess has been developed. You don't have any habits that came to you at birth. I often say that a birth certificate gives people the right to achieve their dreams, but a birth certificate does not give you a set of habits that will ultimately structure your life. Those are built and developed by you.

For example, you weren't born brushing your teeth. You had to develop that habit. Do you ever miss a day of brushing your teeth? Of course not. That's the power of a habit. So, let's look at different habits. Before we consider the habits of Champions, let's look at what *not* to do. Here are a couple of characteristics of really bad habits:

Focus on Money: One of the worst habits that I've seen worldwide is people focusing all of their time and energy on making money. They don't have it, they want it, and they will do anything to get it. When people chase money, they end up broke. Contrary to what you have heard, money is not the root of all evil; the *love* of money is. Loving money will lead to petty (or larger) theft, cheating, gambling, and all kinds of corruptions. Champions are focused on serving others and changing lives not making money. If you serve from a pure heart, money will follow.

Here's another problem with love of money: the law of sowing and reaping. People that are focused on money are sowing the seed of greed everywhere they go. Trust me; that little crop will come up. They will reap their own greed in many situations from employees, clients, vendors, business partners, etc. Unfortunately, this greed reared its ugly head in 2009 throughout our country in the form of billion dollar Ponzi schemes, and you saw what those guys reaped for themselves and their families.

Education Obsession: First, let me say that education is great. I have a degree, and I believe education can serve a clear and fine purpose in our development. But, to see education as a synonym for success is a huge mistake. Getting a diploma is only one step of preparation for life. It doesn't matter whether you're educated or not; you still have to "Find Your Why." You still need to separate from negative influences; you still need to focus daily on changing lives, and all the other things that mark Champions. Always remember that talent outweighs education or a resumé any day.

So, what are Champion habits? Just as you can spot eagles high in the air because of the way they fly, you can spot Champions according to their habits. Here are a few:

Write a Why Card and Read It Daily: This is one of the biggest secrets to success I know. A Why Card is a simple way to capture *why* you are on this earth. Your Why is your compelling reason for living. One of the greatest Champion habits is creating your Why Card and reading it every single day. A Why Card is very basic. Simply write your Why on a 3x5 index card and carry it with you everywhere you go. I recommend that you read it for seven minutes when you get out of bed and again right before you go to sleep. It's a great way to start and end your day plus it will keep you focused on your true purpose. Here's a sample Why Card to get you started:

I am dealing with all the challenges of building my business today, because my WHY is to spend more time with my family, provide for my children's education, and have the finances needed to take regular family vacations and be a mentor to my kids. I am donating/tithing a percentage of my earnings to my church or favorite organization. I am making a difference today as a profit producing, fear demolishing, record breaking, action taking, eye opening, mind blowing, fired up and laser focused millionaire Champion!

How would you feel reading that every morning before you start your day? I guarantee that developing the habit of reading your Why Card will dramatically change your results in every area of your life. With every challenge or obstacle in life that you face, simply face it head on and read your Why Card. Start internalizing your Why in your mind, your heart and your spirit. It will change your life forever, and you will never go back to that point you were at before you found your Why.

Speak Positive Words: I've found that Americans don't understand the power of words like some cultures do. When we speak words, those words take on a life of their own. Just as negative words spoken by our parents have deep power in our lives, so do positive words. You can literally change the environment of your life and develop a champion habit by speaking a blessing to your family, your car, your house, your job, your bank account, your dreams, your sales calls, everything. That means telling yourself the truth!

Tell yourself out loud – "I am a Champion! I expect greatness in my life today! I am a laser-focused, fired-up, action taking champion! I am soaring like an eagle." Bombard yourself with true words constantly. Blast the negative thoughts right out of yourself and your environment.

Choose a Personal Title and Credentials: You can spot Champions by what they call themselves. You don't have to use the same job title and credentials that most people choose. For example, a national sales manager in Dallas has Chief Concierge as his job title. I love that! Most people in his position would just refer to themselves a Sales Manager. What's the difference? The Chief Concierge sees his role and himself as more than just a Sales Manager. Just like some people have BS, MA, PhD after their name indicating the level of education or certification they have attained, why not put WW for Why Warrior or LC for Life Changer after your name? If you think that's silly, then you are not serious about developing Champion habits in life. Instead, you take the easy route of just following the crowd.

My point here is not that Champions make a habit of trying to be different. Rather, Champions know their life is their own. So, they make a habit of designing it. Disregard traditional titles. You know you and your Why better than anyone else so be bold and design your life. Your life is yours to operate so don't base it on someone else or society's job descriptions. Put whatever you want on your business card. After all, it's your way of telling others who you really are.

Read Personal Development Materials: Champions make a habit of reading positive, uplifting, encouraging, and inspiring books, articles, and other materials. However, most people just waste their time with the wrong kind of reading material if they read at all. Just as you are careful about which foods to feed your body, you have to show as much or more care relating to what you feed your mind. That's why Champions only digest those ideas, stories, and challenges that build up rather than pollute their mind.

Join Positive and Faith-Filled Events: While the majority of people are watching TV, Champions make a habit of immersing themselves in motivation by attending live fired-up events. If you desire to become a success addict, then you have to make a habit of eating, drinking, breathing success. Turn off the TV. Go to an event that will empower you to succeed or pop in a CD or DVD that will encourage you.

Giving: If you want to be magnificently successful, then you need to know the one victory secret that all Champions have in common. That one thing is the habit of generous giving. When you sow generosity, you also reap generosity. Similarly, selfish attitudes about money will reap poor results. Stingy people do not become truly successful in life. Champions believe this statement; therefore, they build a habit of giving, giving, giving, and then giving some more.

Now, it's your decision to begin developing new Champion habits. Always remember, you're your habits predict your future so diligently form the ones that will give you the future that you want. It's your life. Be there.

Contact John Di Lemme:
www.ChampionsLiveFree.com

Sandy Harper

Growing up in the countryside of Central Florida, Sandy Harper learned to appreciate the beauty of nature, the serenity of solitude, and the art of enjoying life's simple pleasures. After losing her parents as a teenager, she learned to stand strong in the face of adversity and to fully appreciate her loved ones. She embraces the gift of motherhood that she was miraculously blessed with "later in life" and has a passion for helping others to live in Gratitude, no matter the circumstances. She is the Creator/Coach of Gratitude Boot Camp and the Certified Leader for the Orlando Chapter of the Women's Prosperity Network.

Contact Sandy Harper:
www.SandyHarper.net
Sandy@SandyHarper.net
www.WomensProsperityNetwork.com/Orlando
407.592.4663

Gratitude: The Habit That Will Create the Life of Your Dreams!
by Sandy Harper

Three months before my Mom died, she asked me to sit down at the foot of her bed, a hospital-style contraption that was placed into my bedroom two years before. She had been suffering from cancer for four years when we sat down to talk. I know that she timed it for when she was alert because she knew that she would be leaving soon. I had just turned sixteen and my younger brother had just turned thirteen. The three of us lived in a small yet cozy house in the country, along with my Daddy, who was in his seventies, and my older brother who later joined the Navy when she died.

She always gave me her words of wisdom and on this particular day, she wanted to talk to me about gratitude. "I know that you are losing your parents at a very young age and that you will have to raise your little brother. And I know that we are not leaving you any money at all. Listen closely, Sandy," she said as she gently laid her frail hand upon mine. "Even in the midst of heartache and challenges, there is so much to be grateful for in this world and in your life. You are healthy; you have a lot of great friends. You are strong; you are beautiful and you are smart. You can achieve anything that your heart desires provided that you always have a heart filled with gratitude, possess a positive attitude, are non-judgmental, and are a blessing to others. Hold your head high, no matter what, because you are one of God's creations. And realize that sometimes in life, 'it is what it is' and that is when you fall back on your fond memories and count your past and current blessings to gain the strength to move forward."

After our talk, she began to lose her battle a little more every day. But she never complained...not once. The night before she died, I stopped before entering our room because I heard her talking. She was reciting The Lord's Prayer. Those were the last words that she was to speak. The next day, as she held on to life, I could not bring myself to enter the room to say good-bye although that is what everyone was encouraging. As dusk was approaching, I slowly went to her side. I held her hand, kissed her forehead, and said, "Good-bye Mom. I love you." She passed away a few minutes later.

Three years later, on Christmas Eve, my Daddy passed away in his sleep.

On a cold, breezy day a few days after that Christmas, I sat at their gravesite and made a promise that I would live in gratitude the way that my Mom instructed. Suddenly, I was overcome with the realization that I had the choice to be sad every year during the holiday season or that I could celebrate it every year, and do it in a way that would make fond memories for others to fall back on when they needed strength to move forward.

Throughout my adult years, I have faced much heartache and many challenges: death, divorce, financial worry, the consequences of wrong decisions, the ending of relationships. And during it all, I have maintained a positive attitude coupled with a healthy dose of humor, which is a very critical tool to have as we travel this incredible journey called life.

Late in the first decade of the new millennium, I somehow lost my way and detoured into some unsettling territory. The real estate market had crashed, and along with it went my six-figure income as a real estate agent. Because I was already feeling unfulfilled in that profession, I did not have the heart to put in the time, energy, and effort that it would require to succeed during the rough times, as I had done during down markets in the past. At the same time as the market crashed I gave birth, as a single Mom, and a close friendship came to an end.

While I gave thanks every day for my "miracle" baby, and while I continued to be positive towards others, I spent the majority of my time thinking about and worrying about my misfortunes. I had traveled into the City of Lack and kept visiting and revisiting Self-Pity Park, Blame Bistro, Misery Movies, and Frustration Fashions. It was not an enjoyable place to be and yet I stayed there *for two years*!

At the beginning of 2009, as my 50th birthday was approaching and as my precious baby turned into a little man at the age of three, my Mom's words came rushing back to me and served as a road map which led me back onto Happiness Highway. I stopped focusing on my lack and the challenging place where I was dwelling. I started focusing on what wonderful possibilities and opportunities lay ahead and I began to make gratitude a daily habit. And, my life changed in profound ways.

Not only have I been able to handle those inevitable bumps in the road in a calmer and more positive way, I have also been able to fulfill my life's purpose of helping others to live a life filled with happiness, peace, love, success, and abundance, by creating Gratitude Boot Camp. Through Gratitude Boot Camp, I have the honor and blessing of coaching people on how to make gratitude a daily habit and to develop the skills necessary to move forward in their life journey with excitement, peacefulness, strength, and with specific plans in place in order to reach their ultimate destination.

Gratitude Boot Camp covers twelve topics that give you specific ways to map out your destination to the life of your dreams. Fuel your passion for life by following these directions:

♥ Topic 1 – Gratitude and Awareness ~

Keep a Gratitude Journal – Find one that resonates with you and that makes you feel happy. Sit down every day or once per week (whatever feels better for you) and write down a list of every person and/or event that filled you with gratitude that day/week. Start your day in gratitude by going to www.Facebook.com/GratitudeBootCamp and participating in the "I am/Grateful Project."
Be aware of others. Make it a daily habit to compliment someone, smile at everyone, and to express gratitude.

♥ Topic 2 – Finding your Passion/Purpose ~

Pay attention to what brings you tremendous joy, and what causes you to smile, as you travel throughout your day. This will lead you toward your purpose in life.
Take a quiet hour or two all to yourself where you will have NO interruptions. Turn on some soothing music. Take several deep breaths and ask for guidance towards your purpose. Now, sit with a pen and paper, and start writing words and phrases that pop into your head. Put a big star next to the ones that really cause an emotional reaction.

♥ Topic 3 – Love is For-Giving ~

At the top of a piece of paper, write the words I RELEASE. Then list any and all resentments and hurt feelings that you have towards anyone. Write down all of the negative feelings and then burn that piece of paper. Think about the lessons that you gleaned from the hurtful experience and give thanks for them.

Ask that the other person be blessed in their life.

♥ Topic 4 – Your Thoughts Expand ~
Pick a word to be your "Power Word." The second that a
limiting or negative thought starts to enter your mind, shout your
word out loud (even if it's only in your head). Then, take a deep
breath and count your blessings.
When you find yourself in a challenging situation, take a piece of
paper and write down questions regarding the issue. (Who can
help me with this challenge? What is the lesson I have learned?
What can I do right now to start eliminating this from my life?)

♥ Topic 5 – Watch your Words ~
Replace the word "if" with "when." Instead of "I have to" say
"I get to." Substitute "I need" with "I have or I am."
Eliminate the words "try" and "maybe" from your vocabulary.

♥ Topic 6 – Positive Affirmations ~
Make a list of everything that you want financially, personally,
professionally and spiritually. Now, re-write the list and put it
into present tense, as if it has already come about. You now have
your affirmations. Repeat them several times every day, first
thing in the morning and last thing at night, with feeling and
emotion attached to each one. Repeat the words "I am so
grateful" after several of your affirmations.

♥ Topic 7 – Commitment Leads to Action ~
List five things that you will passionately, unequivocally,
steadfastly commit to with 100% of your being. Keep in mind
that the four areas that you must commit to are 1) yourself; 2)
others; 3) your faith; 4) your work.

♥ Topic 8 – Dreams Do Come True ~
Create a Dream/Vision Board. Go back to the list of everything
that you want. Find pictures/artwork that match up to the item,
event, or person on your list. Place a favorite picture of you in
the middle of a board and surround it with the representations.
Look at your Board every morning and every night and give

thanks for what you see there.

♥ Topic 9 – The Power of Asking ~
    Create opportunities by simply asking for what you want,
    keeping in mind that you never had it to begin with so you are
    not losing anything if the answer is No.

♥ Topic 10 – Action Builds Dreams ~
    Go back to the list of everything that you want. Make a list of
    the action steps that need to be taken under each desired item.
    Do at least one action step every day until they are all completed.

♥ Topic 11 – Facing your Fears ~
    Face a big fear head-on and from that point on, you will be able
    to handle your insecurities with courage. Afraid to fly? Get on a
    plane. Afraid of heights? Jump out of one!

♥ Topic 12 – Give and Receive ~
    Give freely of compliments, encouragement, and praise. Donate
    a portion of the money that you earn. Volunteer your time to a
    charity or charities. Bestow lots of hugs and kisses. And, give
    thanks for ALL of your blessings, it will come back to you in
    magical ways. Receive gifts, compliments, assistance, praise, etc.
    with grace and gratitude and even more will flow into your life.

It is important to make gratitude a habit because your habits
create your life. And a heart filled with gratitude will bring forth the
thoughts that will lead to a life of happiness, peace, success, love, and
abundance, not only for you but for everyone that you meet, know, and
love.

Contact Sandy Harper:
www.SandyHarper.net
Sandy@SandyHarper.net
www.WomensProsperityNetwork.com/Orlando

Darnella Cordier

D arnella Cordier is President and Creative Director of The Third Entity, Inc. The company provides printing, publishing, marketing, book production, website development, e-commerce and Internet marketing.

As a ghostwriter and editor, she has collaboratively written over fifteen books. Darnella's self-publishing workshops have been attended by thousands of people who acclaim her publishing knowledge base as 'the best in the industry.'

Recently she and her business and life partner developed Seven Simple Solutions™, which offers easy ways to provide answers to life's issues and problems. Their first product, 7 Simple Solutions™ Daily Actions Journal has received raved reviews.

Contact Darnella Cordier:
Darnella@SevenSimpleSolutions.com

Seven Simple Solutions ™
Everything You Desire is Waiting for You to Show Up
by Darnella Cordier

There's a door of great mystery;
Single and unchanging,
But the doorkeepers are a many.
One by one. They come and serve.
~ Rumi ~

It is truly an honor to be included in this book amongst such visionaries. You see, I have been told I am a visionary by the clients I have served, but I just couldn't see it. After all, who me? This plain and simple woman? As my mother has told me over, and over, "We do not see ourselves as others see us." I freely offered my professional advice and assistance to people who came into my life to help them achieve their dreams, often in casual conversations. Watching miracles occur in their lives, I now understand the gift I have developed. My visionary talent comes from the foundation gifted by the most loving, compassionate mentors and role models I know – my parents. When I look back at their accomplishments, I understand their achievements were an 'inside job.' My parents somehow knew everything they desired was waiting for them to 'show up' and claim it; from inside their minds and hearts. They had a commitment to daily using specific actions to solve any problems and issues life presented. I call their actions *Seven Simple Solutions ™*. They are:

Solution #1: Gratitude – Be grateful each day for your prosperous life.

Solution #2: Give – Increase your gifts of compassion, love and laughter.

Solution #3: Trust – Acknowledge your intuition.

Solution #4: Open -Experience the wonder of unexpected events.

Solution #5: Listen – Hear the emotions behind words.

Solution #6: Forgive – Make peace with your past.

Solution #7: Imagine –Your visions are real. Live your visions.

When I was a youngster, my parents wanted to get away from loving, meddlesome relatives so my parents could live their lives the way they wanted to. Though grateful for their relatives' support, my parents felt they could have a better life in another town. Not knowing where to move to start a new life, they decided to take an unconventional way to decide where to relocate. They took a map of the United States, pasted to a globe, and spun it. With their hands clasped, index fingers pointing, eyes closed, they stopped the globe. Their combined index fingers landed on the map's seam between the west coast and east coast of the United States. They trusted their intuition and moved from the Midwest clear across the country to New England. My parents knew no one in New England. They sold their properties and businesses. My father left first and found a beautiful house with a large yard. The new house even had a fireplace for Santa to visit! When we arrived, my father led us in a gratitude prayer.

After they became familiar with their surroundings, they looked for employment. My mother took a graveyard shift job as a nurse's aide at a mental hospital for the rich and famous. My father took a job driving a city bus. When my mother arrived home from her graveyard shift, my father left to go to his job.

Through their jobs, they met people from every culture and nationality. I recall they had parties to share their love for humanity. When the guests arrived, each received a warm, loving embrace from both of my parents. The parties were potluck with food representing the various cultures. Sharing this food helped people understand the gift of compassion. The guests told cultural stories sharing in the joy of mutual laughter.

Wanting more security, my parents were open to any unexpected opportunities showing up. My mother listened to people who were passionate when they told her she could do more in her life with a better job. Unexpectedly, she got wind of a job in city government, applied for and got the job. The job was waiting for her to 'show up.'

At the same time, my father decided he could offer more for our family, so he decided to start a maintenance business where he could clean banks in the evening. When time permitted, he took my brothers with him so they could 'learn the ropes.' He gained the reputation of having the best maintenance business. Through the friends my father met on his bus route, he learned he could provide more for our family. He imagined he could be successful in the real estate business. A successful real estate business was there waiting for him to 'show up.' My father left driving a bus and opened a real estate firm. He often gave up his commission to help people achieve the American Dream of owning a home. My father knew his success would come from helping others.

Back to my mother. More job opportunities appeared, but in order to be eligible, she needed more education. She went to college, obtained her degree, and applied for a position as comptroller for a major city's redevelopment agency and was appointed. My mother was the first woman and African-American to hold such a responsible, prestigious job. Her work involved showing compassion as she helped disenfranchised people relocate to better housing.

At the same time, my father and his real estate business partner became the first Africa-Americans appointed to the state's real estate board.

The meddlesome relatives were so proud of my parents' accomplishments that they wanted to visit to see the success with their own eyes. With forgiveness in their hearts, my parents made peace with their past and invited my grandmother to visit. She moved in with our family!

While the instances I explained earlier appear isolated events of daily action solutions, trust me, every day my parents practiced gratitude in big and small ways with prayers and lending a helping hand to those in need. Each day they gave compassion to people they barely knew by offering unconditional love through hugs and laughter. When unexpected events or opportunities appeared often daily, they trusted their intuition and remained open to all possibilities. My parents simply knew achievement required daily imagining, commitment, and love. They lived their visions. Every day, they listened to people who were excited about their potential. When forgiveness was on the horizon, they made peace with their past and moved to that higher plain. Everything was there, waiting for my parents.

Interestingly, just as my parents had, I relocated to a new city to achieve a better life, not knowing anyone in my new location. I wanted warmer weather, and I took a job in a not-for-profit organization helping people. After I became familiar with my surroundings, I developed my part-time business into a fulltime, prosperous career. I, too, have friends and colleagues from all cultures.

So how have I used the Seven Simple Solutions in my life to achieve daily success? I had to take full responsibility and know success is an 'inside job.' To be successful, I had to take into my heart and my consciousness, the attitude of gratitude. I examined where I could be more grateful for my prosperous life. Every day, I survey my life and count amongst my blessings that I have family and friends who love and support me; that I have work I love, and that I am aware of my talents and gifts to help people. My heart tells me to increase giving daily. It just takes nanoseconds to offer compassion and take a can off a shelf in the grocery store when a senior citizen is having trouble reaching it. It is a breeze to laugh with the person who feels silly when they make what they think is a mistake. It feels wonderful to give love and comfort to my friend whose aging mother is dying. When I get that 'funny' feeling telling me to take a different route to a destination, I trust my intuition and take heed. Later the confirmation comes when I hear there was a massive traffic backup on the route I had planned to take.

The Simple Solution of Forgiveness, well, I have to admit is sometimes difficult especially when I feel misunderstood. I had a client who wrote very hurtful comments about me. The remarks burned in my heart. When, I read 'between the lines' and 'heard' the emotions behind her written words, I realized what she was really looking for was compassion for the mistreatment she received from others; not me. I forgave her and me!

As for visioning, I am a big dreamer. Just as many of you have, I imagined the perfect mate to come into my life. Physically, as a tall woman, my superior man must be the proverbial: tall, dark and handsome. He had to have very specific attributes, that of: compassion; understanding me, and adoring my godessness. My perfect mate had to have a formidable intellect matching my insatiable curiosity and appetite for query of all interesting life aspects. Further, he must adorn me with gifts – shallow, I know.

In my vision, I imagined a perfect mate coming from a source beyond my immediate sphere, so I tried Internet dating. The experience was disastrous. Most of the dates wanted one thing, and one thing only. Yup, you know what they wanted. A close male colleague was the ear I needed to share my journey. He patiently listened to my Internet dating search. I even wanted him to participate in my search by meeting the dates. Little did I know, my close colleague was more than the perfect mate for me. You see, I was looking for the mate of my dreams with the attributes I felt would be best for me. Most importantly, tall, dark and handsome. I guess you know by now, he, the one, my superior man, 'showed up' waiting for me to 'show up'. He 'showed up' right in my immediate sphere. Tall, no. Dark, no. Handsome, yes. He is compassionate; understands me; adores the goddess in me; possesses a voracious desire for intellectual pursuits, and ah, the gifts, they are well beyond the physical.

Seven Simple Solutions ™ paved the way for me to 'show up' and to claim my desires.

Practice Seven Simple Solutions ™ every day and your success will 'show up' in the most miraculous ways.

Contact Darnella Cordier:

Darnella@SevenSimpleSolutions.com

Conclusion
by Nancy Matthews

As you read through this book and the stories, inspirations, techniques and strategies shared by the amazing Visionaries with Guts who contributed to this project, you can see that being a Visionary with Guts is a combination of many factors. The common thread within all the messages was the importance of living your purpose (not someone else's), committing to it fully and developing the daily habits that will ensure your success.

Do not let your journey stop here. For some this will be the jumping off point for your leap of faith to find and pursue your passion. For others this will not only be your confirmation that you are on the right path, it will also provide you with the motivation, tools and resources to continue to grow, flourish and prosper. For all, may this collection of wisdom, wit and warmth inspire you to stay committed to being a "Visionary with Guts," to enjoy life's precious moments and joyfully share the message with others.

I encourage you to fight for your dreams, stand up for your purpose and utilize the resources within these pages to take action and turn your dreams into reality!

As I conclude, I must offer special thanks and gratitude to John Di Lemme, my personal mentor, business coach and friend, whose book, *10 Life Lessons On How to Find Your Why NOW & Achieve Ultimate Success,* changed my life by showing me the value of uncovering and living my "Why." He has encouraged me, challenged me and cheered me on and has been a stellar example of being fully committed to thinking, breathing and living your "Why." In tribute to John, I share with you now what it means to me to be a "Why Warrior."

Be a 'Why' Warrior! Your Dream Deserves It!

"W" Know your 'Why' - your purpose, your mission and focus on it daily.

"A" Powerfully choose your 'Attitude' in every moment.

"R" Be 'Relentless' in the pursuit of your Why and Never Give Up!

"R" Be 'Resilient' - Be flexible and deal with what emerges. Learn to 'bounce back' quickly to fight for your Why.

"I" Be 'Inspired' by your Why. When you believe in your Why, can see it, feel it and know it as your reality, inspiration will come that magically moves you forward on the perfect path.

"O" Have 'Objectives' and goals to work towards. Create a plan and stick to it!

"R" Enjoy the Roller Coaster! Life as a Visionary with Guts is filled with opportunities to experience the exhilaration of speeding up to the top of the crest as well as the thrill of the downward slope, knowing that the next turn brings you right back up again.

Free MP3 download of "What It Takes to be a Why Warrior" with Nancy Matthews and John Di Lemme at:

www.WomensProsperityNetwork.com/WhyCall

About Nancy Matthews

Founder of Women's Prosperity Network. Nancy is a National Speaker and Author, with over 25 years of experience in business and legal communities. Referred to as the "Visionary with Guts" for her willingness to move forward in the face of fear, adversity and challenge, Nancy has dedicated her life to bringing out the best in others and truly "empowering" them to live the life of their dreams. As a business owner, parent, and community leader she has mastered the art of being a balanced and happy entrepreneur and it brings her joy to share the keys to success with others. She shares her gift of "word wizardry" and ability to connect with others in providing marketing services to help others effectively deliver their message through her "Magical Marketing Makeover."

Before opening her own business in 2002, Nancy spent 20 years in the legal profession, as an office manager and paralegal for small law firms, which she helped grow to multi-million dollar businesses. Her ability to create and build businesses stems from her solid business skills coupled with an understanding of people, uncovering their needs and providing solutions. Sharing the strategies she has used and developed to build her own business, as well as others, her *Magical Marketing Makeovers* are just that...*Magical*!

The foundation of Nancy's life philosophy is to love the life you live. Right now, in this moment find it perfect. Then from that place of acceptance, create the life of your dreams! She has spent years developing and cultivating her true passion of being of service to others and enjoying each moment, recognizing that the present is just that ... a wonderful gift to be cherished. Her system, Dream Board Secrets, reveals the strategies and secrets she has used to create the life of her dreams, and she invites you to do the same. Visit www.DreamBoardSecrets.com and download her free article "7 Secrets to Revealing Your Purpose, Passion & Power!"

Share your inspiration, triumphs, challenges and victories with Nancy at www.VisionaryWithGuts.com

Contact Nancy Matthews:
Email: Nancy@WomensProsperityNetwork.com
www.WomensProsperityNetwork.com
www.DreamBoardSecrets.com
www.MagicalMarketingMakeover.com
www.VisionaryWithGuts.com